More Building Assets Together

130 Group Activities for Helping Youth Succeed

Rebecca Grothe

Search | *Practical research benefiting children and youth*
INSTITUTE

More Building Assets Together:
130 Group Activities for Helping Youth Succeed

The following are registered trademarks of Search Institute: Search Institute®
Development Assets®, and Healthy Communities • Healthy Youth®.

10   9   8   7   6   5   4   3

ISBN: 1-57482-433-3

Search Institute
615 First Avenue Northeast, Suite 125
Minneapolis, MN 55413
800-888-7828
www.search-institute.org

Library of Congress Cataloging-in-Publication Data
Grothe, Rebecca
  More building assets together : 130 group activities for helping youth succeed / by Rebecca Grothe.
  p. cm.
Includes bibliographical references.
  ISBN 1-57482-433-3
 1. Youth--Conduct of Life. 2.   Youth--Life skills guides. 3.   Values in adolescence. I. Title.
BJ1661 .G77 2002
305.235--dc21
                                                                                          2002013322

Credits
Editor: Kalisha Davis
Book Design: Nancy Johansen-Wester
Production Manager: Rebecca Manfredini

About Search Institute
Search Institute is an independent, nonprofit, nonsectarian organization whose mission is to advance the
well-being of children and youth by generating knowledge and promoting its application. The institute
collaborates with others to promote long-term organizational and cultural change that supports its mission.
For a free information packet, call 800-888-7828.
  Search Institute's Healthy Communities • Healthy Youth initiative seeks to unite individuals,
organizations, and their leaders to join together in nurturing competent, caring, and responsible children
and adolescents. Lutheran Brotherhood, now Thrivent Financial for Lutherans, was the founding national
sponsor for Healthy Communities • Healthy Youth. Thrivent Financial for Lutherans Foundation has
provided Search Institute with generous support.

Table of Contents

Keep Your Hands in Your Pockets

When I was in high school, I spent one summer as a counselor-in-training at Scout camp. My favorite assignment was to teach younger campers how to build and light a campfire. I loved building fires, and I was good at it, so it was great fun to do this. One day I walked with the campers in the woods, teaching about tinder, kindling, and fuel woods and helping them gather a supply of each. I was in the fire circle on my hands and knees, arranging the wood with the campers, when I felt a tap on my shoulder. It was the trainer. She pulled me aside and said: "You've set the stage. Now stand back and keep your hands in your pockets. They've got to learn this by doing it!" These words are in the back of my mind whenever I work with youth. Sometimes the best thing we can do is set the stage for learning, then coach from the sidelines—with our "hands in our pockets."

Just as I've learned to find opportunities to meaningfully engage young people, the activities in *More Building Assets Together* provide an opportunity for youth leaders and teachers to do the same as they set the stage for exploring the developmental assets. I'm encouraging adults to do what I had to do years ago and step back as youth take the lead in discovering the meaning of the developmental assets framework and its implications for their lives.

In this book, I've combined years of experience as an educator and curriculum writer with the many interactions I've had with asset builders across the county and in my own community. As young people experience and discuss the activities, projects, and worksheets in this book, they will grow in their understanding of the developmental assets, learn new skills for building strong relationships, and be challenged to find ways to nurture their own healthy development. Equally important, youth will be challenged to build assets for and with their peers and for and with younger children.

How to Use This Book

The Audience for This Book

Like its predecessor, *Building Assets Together: 135 Group Activities for Helping Youth Succeed,* the activities in this book will be useful to people who are involved with youth in a variety of settings—community youth organizations, clubs, sports teams, congregations, and schools. Communities that used Search Institute's *Profiles of Student Life: Attitudes and Behaviors* survey with their youth will find these activities particularly helpful as they begin to explore and implement asset-promoting strategies.

The activities in this book were designed with 6th- to 12th-grade youth in mind. Certainly, there is a broad range of maturity and interests encompassed in this age range. You will find that some activities are more appropriate for youth younger than yours, whereas others may be a better fit with older youth. Adapt the activities to best meet the needs of your youth and your setting.

How the Book Is Organized

More Building Assets Together is organized around the framework of developmental assets (for a chart of the assets, see page 12). The first chapter contains activities that introduce youth to the concept of developmental assets and invite them to consider the asset framework as a whole. Each remaining chapter presents many activities and worksheets for one of the eight asset categories. You will notice that the worksheets are grouped together at the end of the chapters, preceded by "worksheet helps" that suggest the focus as well as discussion questions for each worksheet.

Throughout the book, the term *group* refers to the entire group of youth in your session, meeting, or class. The term *team* refers to a smaller subgrouping of youth who work together during part of the activity.

Ways to Use This Book

Most of these activities can be completed in less than 30 minutes. Use them in whatever way will best fit your needs. Here are some possibilities:

• **Pick and choose individual activities** as they fit into the ongoing plans for your group. Integrate them into existing objectives, plans, and/or curriculum.

• **Combine several activities** for an entire session or meeting devoted to learning about some aspect of the developmental assets framework.

• **Use activities in intergenerational settings** to help youth and adults explore together the importance of developmental assets.

• **Introduce the eight asset categories systematically,** using several activities for each category once a week or once a month.

• **Encourage youth participants** to select activities to use with peers or younger children.

• **Create a notebook** about the developmental assets for each young person, photocopying the worksheets provided at the end of each chapter.

There are no instant or magical ways to build developmental assets; they are nurtured in numerous ways through a young person's positive relationships with many people. The activities in this resource provide opportunities for engaging in meaningful conversations that can strengthen relationships. Young people will be encouraged not only to learn about the assets but also to understand how they can build them for themselves and with other youth. The real power comes when young people apply what they learn from their group experiences to their own lives.

The activities are designed to be positive experiences for youth. Leaders should be aware, however, that the discussions sparked by these activities might evoke strong feelings and reactions, both positive and negative. Some discussions may be difficult, especially among youth who are experiencing significant stress in their lives. Be sensitive, adapting the activities and questions to your group and your goals. Invite all youth to share their ideas and feedback about the assets and the activities. In this way you can contribute in a significant way to helping them grow as healthy, responsible, contributing members of their community.

Helpful Hints for Working with Groups

If you haven't had a lot of experience working with large groups of people—particularly young people—here are some things to keep in mind as you prepare for the activity, facilitate the discussion, and interact with your audience.

• Know the name of each young person and speak it at least twice during each group meeting. It is ideal to greet and say good-bye to each individual in the group by name. Challenge group members to know each other, and you, by name as well.

• Provide warmth, acceptance, and concern for each individual in your group.

• Find ways to support, affirm, and praise each individual as well as the entire group on a regular basis.

• Provide feedback to individuals or the entire group in ways that are respectful and helpful.

• Think of your meetings as providing a framework for the group to explore the possibilities of change.

• Help your group translate their feelings and experiences into ideas.

• Be ready to learn with your youth. You do not have to be an expert or know all the answers. Do not be too quick to share what you know. Let the group discover new learning together. When you do contribute knowledge or information that you have do so in ways that will enhance the group discussion, not shut it down.

• Be honest as you share about yourself and your feelings. Model acceptance, openness, and trust as you encourage youth to share their feelings and experiences with each other.

• Be a model of good active listening skills.

• As a group, decide on appropriate ground rules for behavior.

• Identify the purposes for each meeting. Is it group building, learning, planning, and/or completing a project? Help the group stay on task, but be careful not to be so task oriented that youth do not have enough time and space for discussion and exploration.

• Let the group wrestle with tough situations and discover how their own resources can pull them through a rough spot. Intervene sparingly.

• At the end of each meeting, help the group summarize and consider new learning to take with them. Identify follow-up action that would be helpful.

• Reaffirm the goals and mission of your group each time you meet.

What's Going on with Your Group?

Carefully observe the interpersonal dynamics in your group each time you meet. As you observe the group in action, ask yourself questions such as:

• Who tries to keep the group interactions on a friendly note?

• Who seems to thrive on conflict and disagreement?

• Are there any youth who provoke others?

• Who seems involved and interested?

• Do any youth seem uninvolved or disconnected from the group? If so, how do other group members treat these individuals?

• Are there any subgroups? Which youth routinely agree and support each other or consistently disagree and oppose one another?

• How are feelings expressed? In addition to those being expressed verbally, look for tone of voice, facial expressions, posture, and gestures.

• Do any group members attempt to block the expression of feelings, particularly uncomfortable ones? How is this done?

Report your observations to the group. Work together to identify ways to create a stronger group. There are many resources available to help you build a healthier group climate. Contact leaders at the YMCA, Boy Scouts, Girl Scouts, 4-H, school counseling centers, or congregations to learn more about being an effective leader of youth groups.

What Are Developmental Assets?

Search Institute has identified 40 positive experiences and qualities—developmental assets—that all of us have the power to bring into the lives of children and youth. The assets are spread across eight broad areas of human development. These categories paint a picture of the positive things that young people need to grow up healthy and responsible. A complete list of the developmental assets is provided on page 12.

The first four asset categories focus on external structures, relationships, and activities that create a positive environment for young people:

Support—Young people need to be surrounded by people who love, care for, appreciate, and accept them. They need to know that they belong and that they are not alone.

Empowerment—Young people need to feel valued and valuable. This happens when youth feel safe, when they believe that they are liked and respected, and when they contribute to their families and communities.

Boundaries and Expectations—Young people need the positive influence of peers and adults who encourage them to be and do their best. Youth also need clear rules about appropriate behavior, and consistent, reasonable consequences for breaking those rules.

Constructive Use of Time—Young people need opportunities—outside of school—to learn and develop new skills and interests, and to spend enjoyable time interacting with other youth and adults.

The next four categories reflect internal values, skills, and beliefs that young people also need to develop to fully engage with and function in the world around them:

Commitment to Learning—Young people need a variety of learning experiences, including the desire for academic success, a sense of the lasting importance of learning, and a belief in their own abilities.

Positive Values—Young people need to develop strong guiding values or principles, including caring about others, having high standards for personal character, and believing in protecting their own well-being.

Social Competencies –Young people need to develop the skills to interact effectively with others, to make difficult decisions and choices, and to cope with new situations.

Positive Identity—Young people need to believe in their own self-worth, to feel that they have control over the things that happen to them, and to have a sense of purpose in life as well as a positive view of the future.

Ideas for Talking about the Assets with Young People

The asset framework appeals to our common sense, but when they first encounter the framework, many youth and adults have a bit of difficulty seeing how it applies to everyday life. Listed below are some simple facts that can help you as your group begins to talk about the assets.

The 40 developmental assets:

- Help you to be healthy, caring, and productive.

- Are validated by years of research involving hundreds of thousands of young people across North America.

- Show that *everyone* can build assets in her or his community.

- Are the positive experiences and characteristics every young person deserves to have in her or his life. Some of this is inside of you, but some of it comes from parents, teachers, friends, and relatives.

- Can make a positive difference in your life.

- Are based on relationships.

- Can help you live a better life and be more successful.

- Can help you make dreams come true.

- Lay the foundation for you to become the kind of adult that you want to be.

The Power of Assets

On one level, the 40 developmental assets represent common wisdom about the qualities of life that young people need and deserve. But their value extends further. Surveys of more than 200,000 students in grades 6–12 reveal that assets are powerful influences on adolescent behavior.

Regardless of gender, ethnic heritage, economic situation, or geographic location, the assets both promote positive behaviors and attitudes and help protect young people from many different problem behaviors. Figure 1 illustrates the relationship between young people's behavior and the numbers of assets they report experiencing.

Figure 1

PROMOTING POSITIVE BEHAVIORS AND ATTITUDES
Our research shows that the more assets students report having, the more likely they are to also report the following patterns of thriving behavior:

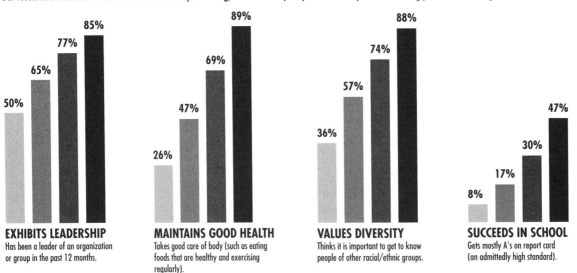

EXHIBITS LEADERSHIP
Has been a leader of an organization or group in the past 12 months.
(50%, 65%, 77%, 85%)

MAINTAINS GOOD HEALTH
Takes good care of body (such as eating foods that are healthy and exercising regularly).
(26%, 47%, 69%, 89%)

VALUES DIVERSITY
Thinks it is important to get to know people of other racial/ethnic groups.
(36%, 57%, 74%, 88%)

SUCCEEDS IN SCHOOL
Gets mostly A's on report card (an admittedly high standard).
(8%, 17%, 30%, 47%)

PROTECTING YOUTH FROM HIGH-RISK BEHAVIORS
Assets not only promote positive behaviors, they also protect young people: The more assets a young person reports having, the less likely he or she is to make harmful or unhealthy choices. *(Note that these definitions are set rather high, suggesting ongoing problems, not experimentation.)*

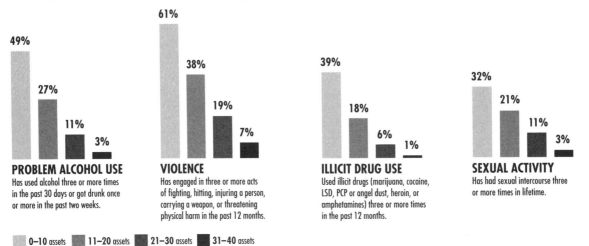

PROBLEM ALCOHOL USE
Has used alcohol three or more times in the past 30 days or got drunk once or more in the past two weeks.
(49%, 27%, 11%, 3%)

VIOLENCE
Has engaged in three or more acts of fighting, hitting, injuring a person, carrying a weapon, or threatening physical harm in the past 12 months.
(61%, 38%, 19%, 7%)

ILLICIT DRUG USE
Used illicit drugs (marijuana, cocaine, LSD, PCP or angel dust, heroin, or amphetamines) three or more times in the past 12 months.
(39%, 18%, 6%, 1%)

SEXUAL ACTIVITY
Has had sexual intercourse three or more times in lifetime.
(32%, 21%, 11%, 3%)

☐ 0–10 assets ☐ 11–20 assets ☐ 21–30 assets ■ 31–40 assets

Take Action

The assets provide a framework that encourages all individuals to take action on behalf of youth. The power of one person to make a positive difference in the life of a young person is strong. It may be easy to assume that young people who experience more assets are more likely to be successful in life, but what many don't immediately realize is that assets are built through relationships. A young person's success isn't just determined by her or his relationships with parents or guardians, but also by interactions with other adults, families, and peers.

Given the power of one person to build assets, imagine what young people experience when they have many people and places in their lives all committed to nurturing and strengthening them by building assets. As we work together to build assets for and with young people, we ensure that they receive consistent messages and treatments. We ourselves benefit because we connect with people who share our ideas, our vision, and our commitments.

Those who work within their organizations to build assets discover and reinforce these perspectives by:

- Focusing on strengthening all youth, more than just a targeted group;
- Renewing an emphasis on intergenerational relationships in the community;
- Viewing youth as participants in the asset-building work, more than simply recipients;
- Involving many more adults in the lives of young people, in addition to those who are professional youth workers and teachers; and
- Recognizing youth as resources and partners in the community and the organization.

In the following pages, you will find the descriptions and worksheets for 130 activities. Understanding that the dynamics of every group can be very different, we encourage you to experiment and develop language or variations that seem more appropriate for your group of young people. This book can assist you as your group begins to explore the possibilities of the developmental assets framework. Good luck!

40 Developmental Assets

This chart shows eight areas of human development and groups the developmental assets by these categories. Percentages of young people who experience each asset were gathered from the administration of Search Institute's *Profiles of Student Life: Attitudes and Behaviors* survey in 318 communities and 33 states.

	ASSET TYPE	ASSET NAME AND DEFINITION	PERCENTAGE EXPERIENCING
EXTERNAL ASSETS	SUPPORT	1. **Family support**—Family life provides high levels of love and support.	70
		2. **Positive family communication**—Young person and her or his parent(s) communicate positively, and young person is willing to seek advice and counsel from parent(s).	30
		3. **Other adult relationships**—Young person receives support from three or more nonparent adults.	45
		4. **Caring neighborhood**—Young person experiences caring neighbors.	40
		5. **Caring school climate**—School provides a caring, encouraging environment.	29
		6. **Parent involvement in schooling**—Parent(s) are actively involved in helping young person succeed in school.	34
	EMPOWERMENT	7. **Community values youth**—Young person perceives that adults in the community value youth.	25
		8. **Youth as resources**—Young people are given useful roles in the community.	28
		9. **Service to others**—Young person serves in the community one hour or more per week.	51
		10. **Safety**—Young person feels safe at home, at school, and in the neighborhood.	51
	BOUNDARIES AND EXPECTATIONS	11. **Family boundaries**—Family has clear rules and consequences and monitors the young person's whereabouts.	48
		12. **School boundaries**—School provides clear rules and consequences.	53
		13. **Neighborhood boundaries**—Neighbors take responsibility for monitoring young people's behavior.	49
		14. **Adult role models**—Parent(s) and other adults model positive, responsible behavior.	30
		15. **Positive peer influence**—Young person's best friends model responsible behavior.	65
		16. **High expectations**—Both parent(s) and teachers encourage the young person to do well.	49
	CONSTRUCTIVE USE OF TIME	17. **Creative activities**—Young person spends three or more hours per week in lessons or practice in music, theater, or other arts.	20
		18. **Youth programs**—Young person spends three or more hours per week in sports, clubs, or organizations at school and/or in the community.	58
		19. **Religious community**—Young person spends one or more hours per week in activities in a religious institution.	63
		20. **Time at home**—Young person is out with friends "with nothing special to do" two or fewer nights per week.	52
INTERNAL ASSETS	COMMITMENT TO LEARNING	21. **Achievement motivation**—Young person is motivated to do well in school.	67
		22. **School engagement**—Young person is actively engaged in learning.	61
		23. **Homework**—Young person reports doing at least one hour of homework every school day.	53
		24. **Bonding to school**—Young person cares about her or his school.	54
		25. **Reading for pleasure**—Young person reads for pleasure three or more hours per week.	23
	POSITIVE VALUES	26. **Caring**—Young person places high value on helping other people.	50
		27. **Equality and social justice**—Young person places high value on promoting equality and reducing hunger and poverty.	52
		28. **Integrity**—Young person acts on convictions and stands up for her or his beliefs.	68
		29. **Honesty**—Young person "tells the truth even when it is not easy."	67
		30. **Responsibility**—Young person accepts and takes personal responsibility.	63
		31. **Restraint**—Young person believes it is important not to be sexually active or to use alcohol or other drugs.	47
	SOCIAL COMPETENCIES	32. **Planning and decision making**—Young person knows how to plan ahead and make choices.	30
		33. **Interpersonal competence**—Young person has empathy, sensitivity, and friendship skills.	47
		34. **Cultural competence**—Young person has knowledge of and comfort with people of different cultural/racial/ethnic backgrounds.	42
		35. **Resistance skills**—Young person can resist negative peer pressure and dangerous situations.	42
		36. **Peaceful conflict resolution**—Young person seeks to resolve conflict nonviolently.	45
	POSITIVE IDENTITY	37. **Personal power**—Young person feels he or she has control over "things that happen to me."	44
		38. **Self-esteem**—Young person reports having a high self-esteem.	52
		39. **Sense of purpose**—Young person reports that "my life has a purpose."	59
		40. **Positive view of personal future**—Young person is optimistic about her or his personal future.	74

Chapter 1

The 40 Developmental Assets

The activities in this chapter will help youth learn more about the developmental assets framework and why the assets are important.

1 ──────────── ## Building Blocks for a Great Life

Focus: Youth enhance their knowledge of the assets.

You will need:

- 40 cubes of the same size (at least four inches) made from small cardboard boxes or upholstery foam
- photocopy of the chart of developmental assets on page 12
- 20 sheets of copier paper in a bright color

Before the group arrives: Cut the photocopy apart so that the assets and definitions are on separate strips; and tape one asset and its description to each block. Place the blocks in a pile in the center of your meeting space.

Set the stage: Say, "Each of you has ideas about the good things young people need in life— about what you need in your life to help you be a caring, responsible, productive member of the community." Ask youth to call out what they think young people need. You may also choose to ask questions such as: "What are the things that inspire you to be your best? Who are the people in your life who are really there for you? How have these people supported you?" Then say: "Search Institute, a research and education organization in Minneapolis, Minnesota, wants to know what children and youth need to be caring, responsible, and productive. Institute researchers have asked more than one million young people about their lives. Based on what young people have told them, the organization has identified 40 experiences and qualities it calls developmental assets. Many of the things you shared earlier are included in the list of assets. *(Recall the things that youth said that are similar to the assets.)* There are others, too. One way to think about these assets is to visualize them as building blocks for a great life. When the adults in your life intentionally try to help you develop and share these strengths we call it *building assets.*"

Step 1: Ask each youth to pick two blocks from the pile, read both assets, and decide which one is stronger in her or his life at this time. Youth keep the blocks that are their strengths and toss the others back in the pile. Youth then choose partners and tell each other why they kept the block they did, who in their life helps them strengthen this asset, and what this person does to build that asset. Repeat this at least three times, each time choosing a new discussion partner and a new block.

Step 2: Take a few minutes for youth to share who in their lives helps them build their assets and the things people do that strengthen their assets. If youth have a bit of trouble, ask them to remember the earlier discussion and the questions that were raised at that time; repeat these questions if necessary.

Step 3: Share more information about the assets as is appropriate for your group. (You may also use the ideas on in the sidebar on page 9, Ideas for Talking about the Assets with Young People.) Include results from Search Institute's *Profiles of Student Life: Attitudes and Behaviors* survey for your community, if you have them, as is appropriate for your group.

Step 4: Ask for a volunteer to represent a child in 6th grade. Point out that even though this young person is trying to build a healthy life, there are many things in our society that work against her or his asset-building efforts. Have the group name some of the forces and factors that work against them, their friends, and younger children (e.g., adults with no time, easy access to drugs, nothing to do after school, negative media attention). Give a sheet of the colored paper to each person who responds.

Step 5: Direct those with papers to wad them up to make a "barrier blizzard." Tell them to stand behind an imaginary line about five feet from the volunteer and then throw their snowballs at her or him on the count of three. Afterward, ask the volunteer how it felt and what he or she thought the chances were to avoid the snowballs.

Step 6: Ask throwers to retrieve their snowballs and stay in place. Say that the typical number of assets a young person reports experiencing is 19. Remind group members how the developmental assets can help protect a young person from negative influences and behaviors. Ask a few participants to work with the volunteer to build a wall with 19 of the asset blocks.

Step 7: Repeat the snowball throw, noting how many snowballs hit the volunteer.

Step 8: Remind group members of their earlier conversations about who has helped them build assets. Point out that a network of positive relationships builds assets. Ask participants to call out the kinds of relationships the child in the 6th grade could have to support her or him and reinforce the asset wall (e.g., teachers, parents, good friends, coaches, religious leaders). Ask eight youth, representing each of the eight asset categories, to come up and stand by the volunteer.

Step 9: Have youth suggest how these people can be most effective (e.g., stay connected with each other, listen to the young person, work to stop the snowball throwers). As suggestions are given, instruct the people up front to act out the group's directions. Point out how these relationships can help a young person build positive qualities of life as well as help protect young people from risky behaviors and other negative influences.

Step 10: Ask youth to form teams of three to address questions such as:
- What will you remember about asset building from this activity?
- It is never possible to stop all the negative forces (snowballs) that bombard us. When negative forces do reach us, what will happen to a person who has few assets and few positive relationships in her or his life? What will happen to a person who has many assets and a strong network of positive relationships?

Beyond the activity: At the end of the activity, save the blocks in large boxes or plastic bags. Use them at other gatherings of youth and adults to spark discussion of individual assets and the framework as a whole. Also, encourage youth to use them when they are teaching younger children about the assets.

2 — May I Have Your Attention, Please?

Focus: Youth create announcements that encourage other youth to build assets.

You will need:
- pencils or pens
- self-stick note pads (about five sheets) per person
- writing paper

Before the group arrives: Write each of the eight asset categories in large print on eight sheets of writing paper. Post the sheets around the room for participants to refer to during the activity.

Set the stage: Ask youth to think of reasons why they should be active asset builders in the lives of their peers and in the lives of younger children. Distribute self-stick notes and pencils or pens, asking group members to write each reason they think of on a separate sheet.

Ask one youth to read what he or she has written, sticking each sheet to the wall or table top as it is read. As each person reports, ask the group to help organize the comments according to the eight asset categories. (This will help the group determine which assets have been addressed and which have not.)

Step 1: Create pairs by asking youth to find another person who is wearing a color that they are wearing. Have pairs of youth write 30-second announcements that will inspire their peers to build assets.

Step 2: Suggest that this announcement will be made over a school public address system, at the beginning of a meeting or class, or as part of a radio broadcast. Ask the group to think about how they can accomplish this. Ask such questions as: "What's the first step? Who do we need to talk to, to get permission? Who would make the announcement?"

Step 3: Allow time for each pair to share their announcement with the group. Once they finish, discuss:

- What are the most effective ways to motivate your peers to do something that you think they should?
- How do we know what messages motivate students?
- What do people need to know about the developmental assets before they are likely to support the idea of asset building?

(3) —————————————— **Alphabet Review**

Focus: Teams compete to compose a list of ideas for building assets.

You will need:
- 40 Developmental Assets List (four copies)
- noisemaker
- pencils or pens
- 24 index cards

Before the group arrives: Label each index card with a letter of the alphabet (omitting X and Z). Create four teams of youth according to birth month (January–March, April–June, July–September, October–December).

Step 1: Distribute six index cards and one copy of the 40 Developmental Assets List to each team. Tell teams to look at their cards, think of asset-building actions that begin with that letter (such as: **A**sk others for help when you need it, **B**e a good listener, **C**are), and write one action on the card. In the next minute they should write an action on as many cards as they can. There might be the temptation for youth to work separately to accomplish this task faster, but encourage individuals in each group to work as a team.

Step 2: After one minute, sound the noisemaker and tell teams that they can pass two blank cards to the next group. After one minute, sound the noisemaker and tell teams that they again can pass two blank cards to the next group. Repeat this each minute until one team has no blank cards left to pass. The first team with no blank cards is the winner. Award them a grand round of applause.

Step 3: Ask each team to choose its three best idea cards and to read these ideas to the entire group. Focus the discussion on:
- What new or unexpected ideas did you hear?
- In what ways could we share these good ideas with others? (Plan to take action on these as appropriate for your setting.)
- Which idea would you make a commitment to try in your own life?

Build Assets in the Lives of Children

Focus: Youth consider how they build assets in the lives of children they know.

You will need:
- markers
- newsprint

Set the stage: As a group, discuss how the process of asset building for and with children begins when babies are born. Identify who the most likely asset builders are as children grow (e.g., parents/guardians, siblings, day-care providers, neighbors, cousins, older relatives, baby-sitters, teachers). On newsprint, list what these individuals do to build assets, adding from these ideas as necessary:
- They provide unconditional love.
- They take care of them and give them clothes, warmth, and food.
- They help them develop their own unique strengths and abilities.
- They teach them the importance of helping others (community service, helping family members, etc.).
- They give good advice and are fair.
- They make sure children have plenty of time with their families and for free play.
- They encourage children to be constructively curious.
- They are good role models.
- They help children learn how to be friends.
- They are easy to talk to and maintain a positive attitude.

Step 1: Form teams of three or four youth. Give each team a sheet of newsprint and several colors of markers. Direct them to draw a large outline of a child on the paper. Inside the shape, they should write the names of children they know and also their ideas of what children need to develop assets—written from the perspective of the child (such as, "I need food and shelter; I need love; or I need to explore").

Step 2: Outside the outline of the child, have groups write tips for older youth and adults on things they can do to build assets for and with children. These might include involving younger children in service projects, encouraging children to dream, modeling how you want children to act, making sure children feel welcomed and comfortable, and teaching children words to talk about their feelings.

Step 3: Display the newsprint creations on a bulletin board where adults and youth will see them. As group members admire each other's work, discuss:
- Who were the asset builders for you when you were younger?
- Why is it important for youth to build assets for and with children?
- How are you building assets for and with younger children?
- If you were writing words of wisdom on a card to the parents/guardians of a newborn baby, what would you say?

The Developmental Assets

Focus: Youth familiarize themselves with the asset framework.

Points to remember: As youth complete this worksheet individually, remind them to star just three of the assets, so that this activity does not become a time for youth to compare numbers of perceived strengths.

As they finish, have youth mark their three starred assets on your copy of the worksheet with tally marks. Report the results of this tally to your group. Begin a discussion by asking questions like:

- What surprised you about the tally from the group? (If you have data for your community from Search Institute's *Profiles of Student Life: Attitudes and Behaviors* survey, discuss how your informal tally compares with the survey results.)
- How can our group learn more about the assets you marked with question marks? (Suggestions: www.search-institute.org; library search; talking with youth and adults about their understanding of the asset.)
- How could you build an asset that you feel you don't have?

Where Are the Asset Builders?

Focus: Youth identify how the organizations they belong to build assets for and with them and others.

Points to remember: If some youth belong to no organization or group, suggest that they name a favorite class at school, a place where they volunteer, or their workplace as they complete this chart. When all have completed the worksheet, have youth share their charts in teams of three. Then encourage a discussion with the entire group by asking:

- Did your teams discover any asset-building actions that the organizations you named have in common? What are they?
- What else could your organizations do to live up to their asset-building potential? Who could do these things?
- Do most youth that belong to your group feel a commitment to strengthen the group? Why or why not?

Review this list of the 40 developmental assets. Which ones are current strengths in your life? Mark your three strongest assets with a star. Then mark with a question mark three assets that you would like to know more about.

1. **Family support**—Family life provides high levels of love and support

2. **Positive family communication**—Young person and her or his parent(s) communicate positively, and young person is willing to seek advice and counsel from parent(s).

3. **Other adult relationships**—Young person receives support from three or more nonparent adults.

4. **Caring neighborhood**—Young person experiences caring neighbors.

5. **Caring school climate**—School provides a caring, encouraging environment.

6. **Parent involvement in schooling**—Parent(s) are actively involved in helping young person succeed in school.

7. **Community values youth**—Young person perceives that adults in the community value youth.

8. **Youth as resources**—Young people are given useful roles in the community.

9. **Service to others**—Young person serves in the community one hour or more per week.

10. **Safety**—Young person feels safe at home, at school, and in the neighborhood.

11. **Family boundaries**—Family has clear rules and consequences and monitors the young person's whereabouts.

12. **School boundaries**—School provides clear rules and consequences.

13. **Neighborhood boundaries**—Neighbors take responsibility for monitoring young people's behavior.

14. **Adult role models**—Parent(s) and other adults model positive, responsible behavior.

15. **Positive peer influence**—Young person's best friends model responsible behavior.

16. **High expectations**—Both parent(s) and teachers encourage the young person to do well.

17. **Creative activities**—Young person spends three or more hours per week in lessons or practice in music, theater, or other arts.

18. **Youth programs**—Young person spends three or more hours per week in sports, clubs, or organizations at school and/or in the community.

19. **Religious community**—Young person spends one or more hours per week in activities in a religious institution.

20. **Time at home**—Young person is out with friends "with nothing special to do" two or fewer nights per week.

21. **Achievement motivation**—Young person is motivated to do well in school.

22. **School engagement**—Young person is actively engaged in learning.

23. **Homework**—Young person reports doing at least one hour of homework every school day.

24. **Bonding to school**—Young person cares about her or his school.

25. **Reading for pleasure**—Young person reads for pleasure three or more hours per week.

26. **Caring**—Young person places high value on helping other people.

27. **Equality and social justice**—Young person places high value on promoting equality and reducing hunger and poverty.

28. **Integrity**—Young person acts on convictions and stands up for her or his beliefs.

29. **Honesty**—Young person "tells the truth even when it is not easy."

30. **Responsibility**—Young person accepts and takes personal responsibility.

31. **Restraint**—Young person believes it is important not to be sexually active or to use alcohol or other drugs.

32. **Planning and decision making**—Young person knows how to plan ahead and make choices.

33. **Interpersonal competence**—Young person has empathy, sensitivity, and friendship skills.

34. **Cultural competence**—Young person has knowledge of and comfort with people of different cultural/racial/ethnic backgrounds.

35. **Resistance skills**—Young person can resist negative peer pressure and dangerous situations.

36. **Peaceful conflict resolution**—Young person seeks to resolve conflict nonviolently.

37. **Personal power**—Young person feels he or she has control over "things that happen to me."

38. **Self-esteem**—Young person reports having a high self-esteem.

39. **Sense of purpose**—Young person reports that "my life has a purpose."

40. **Positive view of personal future**—Young person is optimistic about her or his personal future.

Think about an organization, club, or group in which you participate. What are some of the things you gain from being involved and interacting with other youth and adults? Which asset does the organization, club, or group help build for you and other members? How? Compare your answers to the list of 40 developmental assets. What's similar? What's different?

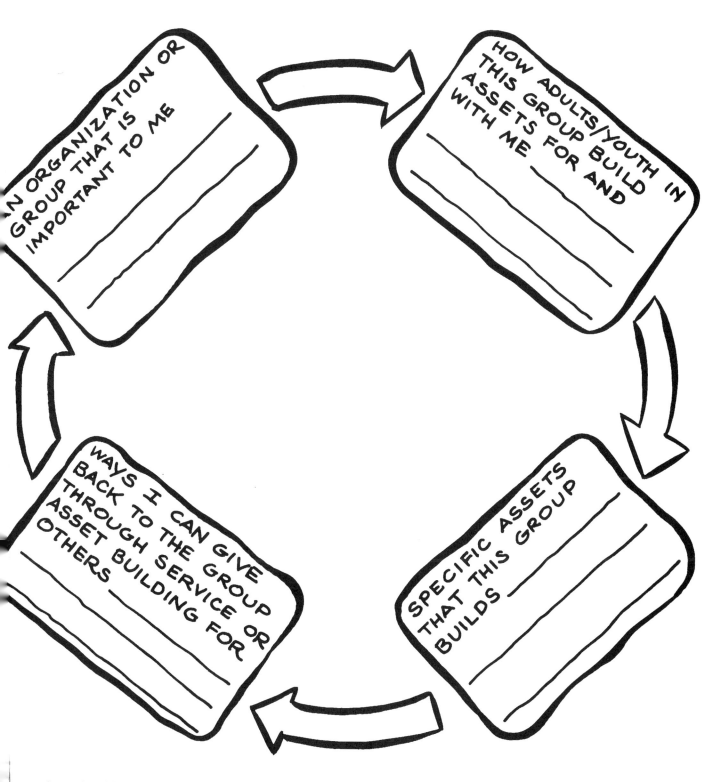

Chapter 2

The Support Assets

Young people need to be surrounded by people of all ages who love, care for, appreciate, and accept them. They need supportive homes, schools, youth organizations, congregations, and neighborhoods. It is important for them to know that they belong and that they are not alone. The activities in this chapter will help youth explore the importance of having and giving support.

7 — Family Photo Fair

Focus: Youth recall times when they have been supported and loved.

You will need:
• family photos

Before the group arrives: Ask each youth to bring one or two favorite family photos, with each photo showing at least two people. Or suggest that youth bring in a picture of someone they think of as "family" (someone who has been supportive, but not necessarily related). Be sure to bring your own favorite photos as well. It may take several sessions to collect all the pictures.

Set the stage: Have each person show her or his photos to the group, answering these questions:
• Who are the people shown?
• When and where was it taken?
• What happened immediately before the photo was taken? What happened after it was taken?
• What were the people talking about before the photo was taken?
• Why do you like this particular photo?

After all group members have shown their photos, spend some time discussing:
• What surprised you most in these stories?
• What did your experiences have in common? How were your experiences different?
• What are some ways that your families give you support, love, and encouragement?
• How do you support, love, and encourage others in your family?

8 — Define It!

Focus: Youth create a definition of *family.*

You will need:
• easel
• markers
• newsprint
• pencils or pens
• writing paper

Set the stage: Begin by asking each individual to write a one-sentence definition of *family.* After a few minutes, ask the group to brainstorm words that describe families. Remember to accept all suggestions without comment, and record each one on newsprint.

Step 1: Form teams of three. Challenge each team to create a one-sentence definition of *family,* based on their individual work and the group brainstorm ideas. Each team should write its definition on newsprint.

Step 2: Post the definitions from the teams, allowing a few minutes for each team to explain its thinking and to answer questions about its work. (Note: Be sensitive to those who have highly dysfunctional families or who draft a definition that seems bleak or disturbing. You might ask group members to comment on the kind of family that they hope to create as adults.)

Step 3: Note similarities and differences in the definitions. Then ask:
• What do families need in order for everyone to be healthy and safe (such as money, food, shelter, health care)? What do families need to stay emotionally healthy (talking to one another, being honest, being supportive)? What other kinds of support do families provide?

- When you think about having a high quality of life (e.g., being happy, having a good job, making a difference) as an adult, how is family part of that dream?
- If a young person is not receiving enough family support, what could he or she do to get more support? How can friends help in this situation?

9 — Idea Storm

Focus: Youth generate ideas for improving school climate.

You will need:
- noisemaker
- pencils or pens
- writing paper

Set the stage: As a group, discuss the meaning of *school climate* and identify the many components that work together in a school to make it feel like a caring and healthy place to be (e.g., supportive relationships between school adults and young people, good relationships among students, safe building and grounds, clear boundaries).

Next, pass out paper and pencils or pens and ask each youth member to briefly describe one problem or situation at her or his school that is working against creating a caring school climate. Collect the papers.

Step 1: Form teams of three and give each team three of the papers. Direct teams to discuss each of the papers for three minutes, recording on the paper as many ways as they can that the writer could work to improve the situation described. Sound the noisemaker every three minutes as a signal for groups to change papers.

Step 2: After teams have responded to all three sheets, gather the group to hear each team report on its work. Ask:
- What challenges do most schools face in creating a caring climate?
- What strengths do schools have on which they could draw to help them improve their climate?
- What is the role of each of the following groups in strengthening a caring school climate: students, parents/guardians, teachers, administrators, other school staff, neighbors, community leaders?

Variation: Ask each young person to describe one strength of her or his school. Teams of three can then think of activities schools could do that build on their strengths and would improve school climate. Also, adapt this activity for other settings such as after-school programs, youth groups, or congregations.

10 — Can We Talk?

Focus: Youth consider the adults who are available to them for support.

You will need:
- four sheets of newsprint
- markers
- self-adhesive dot labels ("sticky dots")
- tape

Before the group arrives: List these categories of people on newsprint (print only three per chart, leaving lots of space between items): my parent(s)/guardian(s); leader or youth worker of my congregation; one of my teachers; my school counselor; a neighbor; my employer (boss); the parent/guardian of a friend; the leader or coach of an organization or team I belong to; a mentor; a family friend; the school nurse; my doctor; other adult. Post the charts around the room. Cut sheets of sticky dots apart so that each youth can have 12 dots.

Set the stage: Tell youth that you will describe situations a young person might face, and that you'd like them to think about which adult they would go to *first* if they needed advice or help such a situation. As you read each situation, pause and ask youth to put one sticky dot next to the adult they would approach *first* for advice or help.

- You want to find a summer job.
- You want to learn a new skill (like salsa dancing or car maintenance), but you're not sure where to start.
- You need money to pay for a school trip.
- You have no desire to get your school work done and you can't figure out why you are not motivated.
- You've been feeling really sick lately, and are afraid it might be from the diet pills that you and your friends are trying.
- You had a huge argument with a friend who now refuses to talk to you.
- You feel like everyone at school is picking on you.
- You've been caught drinking and are going to be kicked off the team.
- You witness a hit-and-run accident.
- A friend tells you he or she is depressed and is thinking about suicide.
- You and your friends want to change the curfew law in your community.
- You are getting a failing mark in a course that is required by the college you want to attend.
- You need to learn to parallel park to pass your driving test.
- You're really nervous about an upcoming audition or tryout.
- You have so much homework that you're about to explode.

Step 1: After you finish this marking activity, invite youth to help you tally the number of dots next to the name of each person listed on the charts.

Step 2: Reflect on the results, asking:

- Why do you think some of the adults listed on the charts have more dots than others? What does an adult do or say that makes it easy to approach her or him for help and advice? What does an adult do that makes it difficult?
- How many different places did you put a dot? How do you feel about the number of supportive adults in your life inside and outside your family? How could you increase the number?
- In what ways do you show appreciation for those who give you support?

11 ──────── **Neighborly Advice**

Focus: Youth offer suggestions for healthy neighborhood relationships.

You will need:
- index cards (or paper)
- pencils or pens

Before the group arrives: Write each of these skit starters on a sheet of paper or index card:

- Today after school, you watch your five-year-old sister and her friend. You take them with you to help rake your neighbor's lawn. After a while, you notice the huge bunch of flowers they are carrying—picked from your neighbor's garden. What do you do now?
- When you got off the bus last Thursday, you noticed people carrying boxes into the apartment two doors down. It's Monday now, and there were two kids you didn't know playing in front of your building after school. What do you do now?
- The woman who lives next door is a widow. Her husband died last summer. You try to be friendly when you see her, and she always wants you to stop and talk. Some days, you just don't have time to visit with her. Today is one of those days. What do you do now?

Step 1: Form three teams and give each team one of the skit starters. Challenge them to plan a skit that shows a course of action that would be a positive experience for everyone involved in the situation. Allow about 10 minutes for teams to work, then ask each team to present its skit.

Step 2: Ask the following:
- Was it challenging to think of solutions that are positive for everyone involved? Why or why not?
- What hurts or gets in the way of positive relationships in your neighborhood?
- What are the three most important things that people of all ages can do to create and maintain a caring neighborhood?

 12 ———————— **Hall Talk**

Focus: Youth consider how what they say affects school climate.

You will need:
- index cards in three colors
- pencils or pens
- white index cards

Before the group arrives: Write each of these situations on a white index card:
- I see a basketball player who hurt her knee in the last game. She's walking with a cane. I say . . .
- I meet a friend who has a new haircut that is way too short. I say . . .
- I run into a kid whom I don't recognize and he drops his books. I say . . .
- My locker is jammed and I am late for English. I say . . .
- A friend gave a wrong answer to a question on the oral quiz in math class and feels bad about it. I say . . .
- A classmate says something that I know is a slam against me. After class I say . . .
- I see someone I don't know really well being pushed around by a bully. I say . . .
- I'm running an errand for the coach, and a teacher asks me why I'm not in class. I say . . .
- A boy or girl asks me to a dance, but I really don't want to go with her/him. I say . . .
- I need to use the office phone to call my mom, but the new secretary says, "Use the pay phone." I say . . .

Set the stage: Give each youth one blank colored index card, making sure that the three colors are distributed evenly among your group. Tell youth that they will take turns drawing a situation card, reading it aloud, and then calling out one of the three colors of cards. Youth who have a card in the color named stand and give a possible response to the situation.

Step 1: After each situation and possible responses, ask the rest of the group to choose the responses they feel would be most likely to improve school climate in the hallways and classrooms.

Step 2: Ask youth the following:
- How do the things people say to each other affect school climate?
- What can be done to encourage youth and adults in school to be more positive when they talk to each other and about each other?

13 ——————— **Parent/Guardian Involvement Reminders**

Focus: Youth discuss ways to increase parent/guardian involvement in their education.

You will need:
• index cards
• markers
• newsprint
• self-stick magnetic tape

Set the stage: Ask youth: "What do your parents/guardians do that lets you know they care about your education? What things do parents/guardians do that are not helpful in supporting your education?"

Continue the discussion by asking: "What are other things that parents/guardians could do that would help a young person's education?" As you discuss, make a list on newsprint of things that parents/guardians can do to be involved in their education in positive ways. For example, talking about what happened in school each day, helping with homework, going to parent-teacher conferences, voting in school-related elections, volunteering at the school, asking how they can help if you aren't getting the grades you want, and sending notes of encouragement to teachers.

Step 1: Invite youth to choose one idea or activity to suggest to their parents/guardians. Pass out index cards and markers for youth to use to make a miniposter with their reminders. Show them how to attach a strip of magnetic tape to the back and encourage them to put the miniposters on their refrigerators at home.

Step 2: Discuss the following questions:
• How will your parents/guardians or other adults at home react to this reminder? What can you do to have a positive discussion about this?
• What are the advantages of having a parent/guardian who is actively helping you succeed in school? What are the drawbacks?
• What advice would you give to parents/guardians who are new to your school?
• What advice would you give to a friend whose parents/guardians are not supportive of her or his activities?

14 ——————— **Virtual Shadow Day**

You will need:
• digital or video cameras
• newsprint

Note: This activity may take several sessions to complete.

Before the activity: Check with school leaders to secure necessary permission for youth to do this activity. Be sure to have the technology necessary for the activity. Or as an option, youth could produce a picture book or photo album.

Set the stage: Comment that it is difficult for many adults to imagine what it's like in school today. Note that many companies host "shadow days" to give young people the opportunity to visit with a professional (usually for a day) and see what it's like to do their job. Ask youth what they would show or do with their parents/guardians or other caring adults if they could plan a "shadow day" for them at school. Record the key responses on newsprint:
• What would most parents/guardians expect to see? What would many parents/guardians be surprised to see? Why?
• Where would parents/guardians feel comfortable? Where would parents/guardians feel uncomfortable? Why?
• What questions do you think parents/guardians would ask?
• What do you wish parents/guardians understood about your life in school?

Step 1: Suggest that an actual shadow day might not be possible for all parents/guardians, so you are going to create a "virtual" shadow day, producing a short video or computer slide show to help parents/guardians get a feel for the school day. Discuss what steps your group needs to take, such as getting necessary permission from teachers, administrators, or other youth.

Step 2: Decide if youth will take turns showing the finished product to their parents/guardians at home, or if parents/guardians will be invited to join youth for a viewing session. If your group is large or represents different schools, you may want to divide youth into teams to produce several virtual shadow day presentations.

Step 3: Decide on the key scenes and have pairs of youth volunteer to use a video camera or digital camera to record each one. Afterward, assist youth as needed to edit the segments into a video or computer slide show, adding other graphics, sound effects, questions on-screen, and music as creativity suggests.

Step 4: When the virtual shadow day video is finished, view it as a group and plan discussion questions to ask after parents/guardians see it, whether individually or as a group.

15 — Back-to-Back Answers

Focus: Youth practice answering questions about their school experience.

You will need:
- masking tape
- pencils or pens
- writing paper

Before the group arrives: Cut sheets of writing paper into fourths. Each youth will need one piece.

Set the stage: Ask youth to close their eyes and think about what happens at the end of a typical school day, answering these questions silently:
- Do you go home after school or to some other place?
- Who are you with after school?
- What do you usually do after school?
- What time is it when you first see your parent/guardian or some other caring adult in your household?
- What questions about school do you usually hear from this parent/guardian or other caring adult?
- Do parents ask the right questions? Are there questions they could ask to show how much they care?

Step 1: Ask youth to open their eyes and write one question about their school day that they commonly hear from parents/guardians on a slip of paper, folding it so no one else can see it.

Step 2: Gather and mix the questions. Tape one to the back of each youth without telling her or him what it says. Form pairs. Instruct one person to be the "youth" and the other to be the "parent/guardian." The "youth" looks at the question on the "parent/guardian's" back, reads it silently, then answers it out loud. The "parent/guardian" gets two tries to guess what the question is. Partners then switch roles.

Step 3: After the activity, discuss some of these questions:
- What information about school is important to share with parents/guardians?
- Do you ever feel like you don't want to talk to your parents/guardians about school? Why or why not?
- What could parents/guardians do to improve their communication with you about school? What could you do?

16 ———————————— **Honor Roll**

Focus: Youth honor the contributions that other adults have made to their lives.

You will need:
- camera (or ask each youth to bring a photo of an adult—other than a parent/guardian—who is important to her or him)
- construction paper
- markers
- newsprint
- scissors
- staplers
- tape

Note: This activity may take more than one session.

Set the stage: Invite youth to think of adults—other than their parents/guardians—who are important to them. Ask the group to list the ways that these other adults have shown support to them. Record them on newsprint.

Have each young person identify one such adult in her or his own life and imagine an award that could be given to this person (such as Best E-mail Sender, Most Positive Outlook, Giver of Great Advice about Cars, Most Fun to Play Cards With, Friendliest Face in School, or Most Encouraging). If there are youth who cannot identify any adult for this exercise, challenge them to think of the kind of support they wish they could have, make an award for that, and attach it to a drawing of an adult labeled, "Could you support a young person in this way?"

Step 1: Create a bulletin board display that honors these important adults. Ask youth to take photos of the adults they admire or use photos they've brought with them. Post the photos and make "award medals" from construction paper to announce the award and tell one example of what this person did to earn it. Ask a few youth to cut large letters to spell out "Honor Roll."

Step 2: After the bulletin board display is complete, discuss:
- Would any of these adults be surprised to find their picture on this bulletin board? Why?
- How do you let these adults know that you appreciate the support they give you? Why is this important?
- How do others let you know that the support you give is appreciated?

17 ———————————— **Long-Distance Support**

Focus: Youth produce a list of ways to keep in touch with those in their support network.

You will need:
- markers
- newsprint
- writing paper

Set the stage: Introduce the focus of this activity by asking youth to share the names of people who support and care for them even though they don't see them very often (twice a month or less). Ask:
- How do you know that these people care about you even though you are not together in the same place very often?
- Are there people whom you support, even though you aren't with them very often? How do you do this?

Step 1: Form teams of three or four. Announce that in each team the youth sitting closest to the door will be the recorder and the one who is the oldest will be the timekeeper. Tell groups that their assignment is to come up with as many ideas as possible for keeping in touch with supporters who are not with us often. They will have five minutes.

Step 2: Ask each recorder to report to the entire group. The first recorder reads the list of ideas from her or his team. Write the ideas on newsprint as this recorder reports. Remaining recorders read only new ideas (no repeats).

Step 3: As you close, ask each young person to tell which idea he or she will try during the next week. Plan for a follow-up conversation to hear how they did.

Variation: Ask youth to write a commitment they'd like to make on a sticky note that they can display at home as a reminder.

Your Cheering Section

Focus: Youth recall caring adults who provide support and encouragement.

Points to remember: If youth have difficulty thinking about which adults to identify on the worksheet, spend a few minutes helping them recall the events of the past week or so: What adults did they have contact with—at home, school, work, in the neighborhood, in your congregation? Which ones let them know they cared?

After youth complete the worksheet, ask each one to choose one adult to present to the group. When all have finished, ask:
• What is your favorite way to have someone show you they support and care for you?
• How big a cheering section does each person need?
• If you don't like the size of your cheering section, how can you increase it?
• Whose cheerleader are you?

Block Party!

Focus: Youth plan components of a neighborhood

Points to remember: Before the activity, check to see if your community or neighborhood has scheduled a block party and find out how the youth's ideas might become part of the planning. If no such gathering is planned, consider the feasibility of the youth hosting a gathering, using the ideas from their sheet.

After youth complete the worksheet, ask:
• Have you ever attended a block party or other neighborhood gathering? If so, who did the planning? What ages of people attended? What was the best part?
• Do you think block parties can improve the caring climate of a neighborhood? Why or why not?

Stir Up a Caring School

Focus: Youth take an inventory of how they are connected with others in their school community.

Points to remember: After youth complete the worksheet, ask each individual to report which two groups he or she has the most conversations with and which two he or she has the fewest conversations with. Tally the responses of the group, and report back. Ask:
• Did the group's results surprise you? Why or why not?
• What is the value in friendly connections with many different groups during the day and during the week? What is the disadvantage?
• How can you become more aware of those around you at school and connect with them in caring and meaningful ways?

Support from School

Focus: Youth analyze their experience of support in various parts of school life.

Points to remember: If youth are challenged or confused by the scoring task, explain that places that feel supportive are places where the adults or other youth make a person feel comfortable or "at home." They are welcoming and a person looks forward to going there.

When the worksheets are complete, ask small teams to compare their ratings. Ask:
• Which areas received the highest scores for a good climate? What other people are in these areas when you are? What happens there? What is said there?
• Which areas received the lowest scores? What other people are in these areas when you are? What happens there? What is said there?
• Who seems to have the most influence on the climate of a place?
• How can you help a person who is creating a negative climate understand her or his role in shaping a better, more caring school climate?

I Wish We Could Talk about . . .

Focus: Youth identify conversation topics that are important to them.

Points to remember: After youth complete the worksheets, ask:
• What are the chances that you and a parent/ guardian or other caring adult at home will be able to talk about the topics on your list?
• What could you say to convince a parent/ guardian or other caring adult at home to complete the other half of the sheet?
• What is the best advice you can share with other youth for talking about challenging topics at home?

Neighbor Search

Focus: Youth find out information about those who live around them.

Points to remember: This worksheet can be started during your group meeting, but may need to be completed afterward. During your session, ask youth to fill in as many squares as they can. Encourage youth who live in the same neighborhood to share information.

After youth are finished, offer some treats as prizes for things such as most squares filled, fewest squares filled, complete vertical rows, complete diagonal rows, and so on. Ask:
• Which squares were hardest to complete? Which were easiest?
• Look at the spaces you could not fill. Which ones do you wish you could? How could you find adults who fit those descriptions?
• What tips do you have to share with the group on how to become better acquainted with neighbors?

Everyone needs cheerleaders. It doesn't matter if we are athletes or not, we all need people who care about us, encourage us to do our best, and support us when we struggle. Think of people who do these things for you as your very own cheering section. Who is in your cheering section? Write their names on the caps. What do they do to let you know they care? Write some of the things they do on the things they are waving. As you complete this sheet, think about the people you cheer for—which friends or family members would draw you in their cheering sections?

In many communities, block parties are a longtime tradition. (Communities that have rural townships instead of city blocks have "block" parties, too!) Neighbors gather for food, fun, and games, and get to know each other better. If you were on the planning team for a block party with and for your neighbors, what theme would you choose? How about food, entertainment, and games? How would you invite or encourage neighbors to come? Use this planning sheet to get started.

Title or theme of the party: _____

Time of day: _____

What we'll eat: _____

The music we'll have: _____

Contests and games we'll play: _____

_____

Other ideas: _____

_____

How we will invite and encourage people to attend: _____

_____

What it will cost: _____

Lots of ingredients work together to create a school climate that's fun, supportive, and positive for all students. The relationships you have with other youth at school are important to the mix. Mark the chart below to show how often you interact with each of these different groups. What would you like to change in your mix?

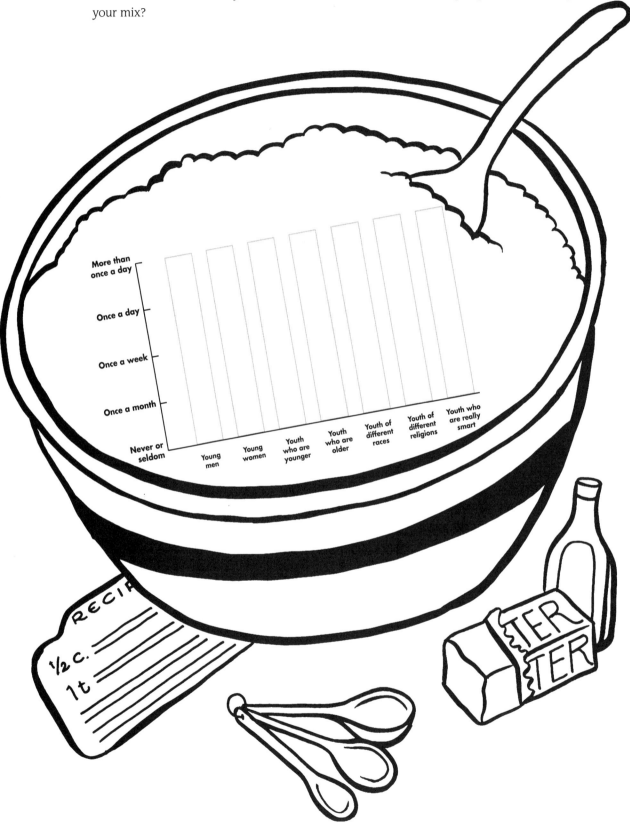

"Climate refers to how teachers, staff, and other students treat each other. What's the climate like at your school? Where do you sense the strongest support and care from adults and other students? Where do you feel "at your best"? If you had the choice, where would you spend most of your time at school?

Consider each of the places labeled on this blueprint. Rate each one with your experience of the climate there. Assign a rating of 1 through 5, using 1 to mean "the worst possible climate for me" and 5 to mean "this is one of the places I like best at school." Write the score for each area on the blueprint. (If you don't see your favorite class or activity, write it in.)

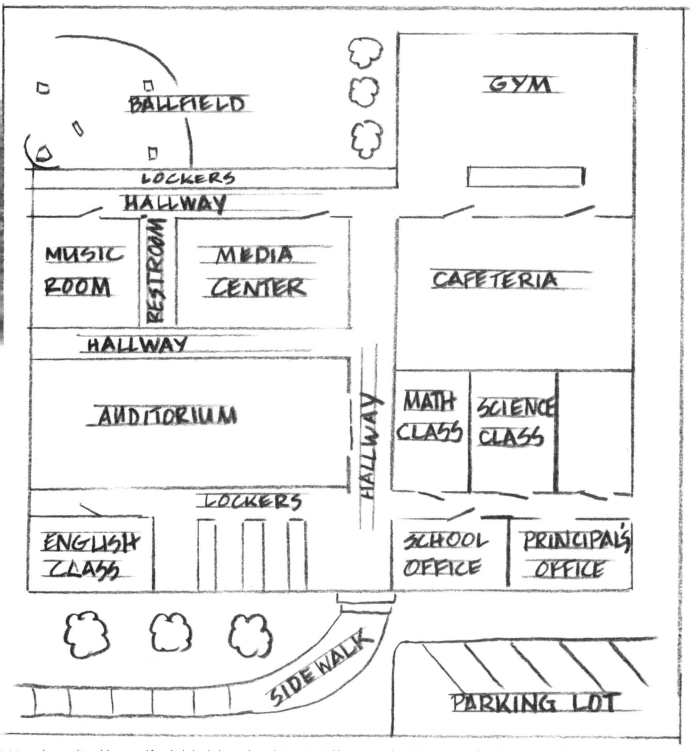

Communication with your family is essential, but it's not always easy. Even in the most caring families, certain topics are avoided. In all families, there are time pressures that make it a challenge to sit down and talk. What topics do you wish you had more time to talk about with your parents/guardians or other caring adults at home? Fold this paper in half. Write the topics you'd like to discuss on one side. Ask a parent/guardian to fill in topics on the other side. Compare your lists. How can you begin one of these conversations?

Who are your neighbors? What do they contribute to a safe and enjoyable place to live? Look at the chart below. Fill in names of people who live in your area who fit each description. You can't use the name of anyone who lives in your house, and you can only use each name twice! If you have trouble with this, take some time to make connections with the people around you.

HAS A GREAT SMILE	KNOWS HOW TO FIX A FLAT	WILL HELP IF I'M LOCKED OUT	HAS NO CHILDREN LIVING AT HOME
IS A GRANDPARENT	LIKES TO CHAT	BAKES TASTY TREATS	ALWAYS HAS TIME TO LISTEN
WAVES FROM HER/HIS CAR	COMES TO GAMES OR CONCERTS AT SCHOOL	HAS CHILDREN YOUNGER THAN I AM	HIRES YOUTH TO DO CHORES
BUYS FUND-RAISER ITEMS	KEEPS CALM IN EMERGENCIES	KNOWS GOOD JOKES	WALKS OR BIKES FOR EXERCISE
KNOWS HOW TO BUILD THINGS	KEEPS AN EYE ON WHAT'S GOING ON	RECYCLES	DOESN'T LIKE NOISE LATE AT NIGHT

Chapter 3

The Empowerment Assets

Young people need to feel valued and valuable. This happens when they feel safe, when they believe that they are liked and respected, and when they make positive contributions to their families and communities. The activities in this chapter encourage youth to consider the importance of feeling valued and safe and to explore ways to be responsible and contributing members of their families and communities.

24

Ask Us a Question

Focus: Youth offer advice to adults on more effective communication with young people.

You will need:
- markers
- newsprint
- pencils or pens
- tape (or an easel)
- writing paper

Before the group arrives: Check with your community newspaper and the editors of newsletters for schools, congregations, and other organizations to see which would like a list of conversation starters that adults can use with youth.

Set the stage: Ask youth: "Think about adults who make you feel like you are a worthwhile person. What do they say? What do they ask?" Record responses on newsprint.

Then ask: "Think about adults who make you feel worthless or seem not to care. What do they say? What do they do?" Record responses on newsprint.

Comment that adults who don't have youth living with them often don't know what to say or ask when they have the opportunity to talk with a young person. Suggest that your group is in a good position to offer advice and suggestions to adults about how to get a conversation started.

Step 1: Form teams of youth who are wearing the same color of socks. Include a "no socks" group. Ask each team to make a list of five phrases they really like to hear adults say to them and five questions they wish adults would ask them.

Step 2: Ask each team to share its list, and work to create a single list of phrases that youth like to hear and questions they wish adults would ask them.

Step 3: Tell youth which newspapers or newsletters are interested in publishing their list, and ask for volunteers to help deliver or mail the information.

25

Ask So They Will Say Yes

Focus: Youth learn key principles in recruiting others to help with projects.

You will need:
- markers
- newsprint
- tape

Before the group arrives: Write each of these steps on a separate sheet of newsprint (listed in order below):
- Describe what needs to be done—the task, when and where it will be done, and how long it will take.
- Ask people face-to-face. Describe the task. Give them time to think about it.
- Make sure that volunteers have good instructions and the right tools and supplies for the job.
- Help volunteers get to know each other as they work.
- Ask volunteers for suggestions to improve the project.
- Celebrate! Thank everyone who helps.

Post the six charts around your meeting area.

Set the stage: Ask youth: "How have you helped someone lately (this includes volunteering)? Have you ever been asked for help? How did that make you feel? Was it a good experience?

Tell youth that there is an art to recruiting volunteers for a project in a way that is respectful of people's time and more likely to get a positive response. Once volunteers are in place, it takes good leadership skills to make a project go smoothly. Point out the charts posted around your space. Explain that these are the steps that many successful project leaders have used. As the group to arrange them in correct order.

Review each step, asking for examples from youth who volunteer of what each step could "look like." (For example, for the fourth step, name tags may be provided or introductions made by the leader as each new volunteer begins.) Youth who haven't volunteered might contribute by saying what would inspire them to get involved.

Step 1: Form three teams, according to first letters of last names (A-H, I-P, Q-Z). Assign each team one of these scenarios and challenge it to prepare a short skit to illustrate how the six steps might be carried out. Use these scenarios or others that fit your community: recruit some one to help with the decorating committee for a class party; recruit someone to help coach pee wee soccer; recruit someone to help raise money for a park renovation project; recruit someon to help organize a neighborhood block party.
Step 2: After the skits are performed, discuss:
• Which of the six steps seems easiest? Which is most challenging? Why?
• How could you use this information to improve a volunteer assignment you are doing right now?

26 ——————————— How Safe Do You Feel?

Focus: Youth express their feelings about safety.

You will need:
• markers
• newsprint
• tape (or an easel)

Note: This activity may remind students of negative experiences (e.g., an abusive home environme. school incident, or act of violence). If you are concerned about your ability to deal with students' feelings about such situations, check in with a school counselor, social worker, or someone else w experience in this area.

Before the group arrives: Write each of these phrases on a separate sheet of newsprint: Completely Safe and Not Safe at All. Clear a long space in your meeting area and hang one chart at each end of the space.

Set the stage: Introduce the activity by discussing with youth what people mean when they s a place is or is not safe. Record their criteria for determining a "safe" place and a "not safe" place on newsprint.

Step 1: Comment that few places are completely safe or completely unsafe. Point out the are you have cleared and the charts at each end. Explain that this is a continuum, and that as yo name a place, each youth should move to the place along the line that describes the degree t which he or she considers that place safe or unsafe. Name these places, adding details as necessary to make them more applicable to your community:
• Four blocks closest to their school
• Where they live
• The neighborhood around their home
• Where they work
• The state, county, or country they were born in
• Their school during the school day

- Their school during after-school activities
- A street in a nearby city at 1:00 A.M.
- A local movie theater
- A local ice rink or other sports facility
- The park closest to their home
- An interstate highway at rush hour

Step 2: After each item, ask for volunteers to tell why they chose to stand where they did (being careful not to single anyone out for their choices).

Step 3: When all items are finished, discuss:
- Who affects how safe or unsafe a place is?
- What can individual youth do to make a place safer?
- What can community leaders do to make a place safer?
- What can young people do to be safe in an unsafe place?
- Who can you talk to about situations like this?

27 Safety Lesson

Focus: Youth plan presentations on safety issues for younger children.

Note: This activity may take more than one session.

You will need:
- markers
- newsprint
- other materials identified by small teams

Before the group arrives: Meet with the leader of a group or class of younger children. Arrange a time for your youth to make a 10-minute safety presentation to them. Or invite a young person in your group to help make the arrangement—he or she may have a younger sibling in a class that the group could work with.

Set the stage: Invite youth to think back to their childhood. Ask: "What safety lessons do you remember from when you were a young child? What safety lessons do you wish you would have had when you were a young child?"

Explain that they are going to make a 10-minute safety presentation to a group of children; tell them the ages of the children and the size of the group. As a group, discuss and decide on a topic that seems most important for children in your community at this time, such as fire safety, bicycle safety, playground safety, or stranger safety.

Step 1: Plan the three key messages that should be presented. Brainstorm ways to present these messages most effectively. Ask youth to volunteer for key tasks such as researching the topic, preparing a script, preparing visuals, or leading activities with children. Make sure each member of the group has a role and a responsibility. (If your group is large, have smaller teams each prepare and give a presentation.)

Step 2: After the presentation, take time to discuss:
- What new information did you learn about this topic as you prepared the presentation?
- What did you learn from the children during the presentation?
- How does it feel to be in the role of teacher?

How Do We Rate?

Focus: Youth hear about research on youth volunteerism and compare it with their own participation.

You will need:
- markers
- newsprint
- pencils or pens
- tape
- writing paper

Before the group arrives: Prepare five newsprint pages with this information, but do not post them:
- **59% of teenagers volunteer.**
- **The average youth volunteer gives 3.5 hours per week.**
- **Most youth volunteer hours are given to these kinds of activities:**
  - Religious: 16%
  - Youth development: 13%
  - Education: 13%
  - Informal volunteering: 13%
  - Environment: 8%
  - Human services: 7%
  - Health services: 6%
  - Arts, culture, and humanities: 6%
- **Reasons youth give most frequently for volunteering:**
  - Feeling compassion toward people in need
  - Doing something to help a cause that is important to them
  - Believing that if they help others, others will help them
- **Benefits of volunteering that youth name:**
  - Do better in school
  - Learn about career options
  - Learn to respect others
  - Learn to be helpful and kind
  - Understand people who are different
  - Develop leadership skills
  - Be a better citizen

Step 1: As youth arrive, distribute paper and pencils or pens, telling them that you are conducting a survey about youth volunteers. Read the following questions and ask youth to write responses on their paper.
1. Have you done any activities as a volunteer during the past month? (Yes or No.)

Note: Youth who answer no can stop writing at this point or see alternate activity.

2. During the weeks that you volunteer, about how many hours per week do you do volunteer work? (a number)
3. Where do you do most of your volunteer work? (place)
4. Why do you volunteer?
5. What good things are added to your life because you are a volunteer?

Step 2: Enlist youth to help you tally the responses of the group. Calculate the percentage of youth in your group who volunteer for the first question (number of yes responses divided by total number of youth). Calculate the average number of hours for the second question (total number of hours divided by number of youth who volunteer).

Step 3: Post the charts with the results of national research on youth volunteers that was completed by Independent Sector. Look at each result, comparing it with your group's result. Mark the chart to show where your group is similar to and different from the national survey.

* Source: *Vounteering and Giving among Teenagers 12 to 17 Years of Age* (Washington D.C.: Independent Sector 199

Step 4: Discuss the following:

• Are there any surprises in the national information? Are there any surprises in the information from our group?

• How would you explain how our results compare with the national survey?

• Should volunteer service be required by schools? Why or why not?

Alternate activity: Ask youth participants who have not served as volunteers to consider the following questions: What are some of the ways they help others in their community? Are they interested in serving as a volunteer? If so, what would they like to do (examples include: taking care of animals, working with younger children, collecting canned goods for a local food shelf)? If not, why? Ask youth to write down some of their interests on a sheet of paper and agree to help them find volunteer opportunities that they can get involved in. Or have a list of volunteer opportunities prepared.

29 ——————— **Tell the Press**

Focus: Youth compose media stories about positive youth activities.

You will need:
• community newspaper(s)
• computer and printer
• pencils or pens
• sample press release (see page 42)
• writing paper

Before the group arrives: Get information from your community newspaper(s), radio station(s), and/or television stations about how to submit a press release or feature story. Cut stories from your community newspaper(s) about events for children, youth, or families that have taken place or are happening in the future. Or if your group meets regularly, ask youth to bring clippings from home.

Set the stage: Discuss with the group information about youth that they have seen or heard recently in local newspapers, radio, or television. Ask if the news seemed positive or negative.

What Is a Press Release?

A news or press release is used to provide information to the media. By informing our local media contacts, you can encourage reporters to cover stories that focus positively youth. Here are some basic rules to follow preparing every press release:

A press release should be no longer than two pages in length unless more space is absolutely essential to tell your story. You need to keep your account simple and straightforward. Try to avoid jargon, as well as complex and nonessential details. All news releases answer five basic questions: who, what, where, when, and how. Always include contact information. At the beginning of your press release, list a contact name and phone number so that a reporter can call if he or she needs more information. At the end of the press release,

you can include specific details about your group or organization.

• Always include a date at the top of the release to convey the time sensitivity of the story.

• Use a headline. The headline summarizes the information in one or two lines and grabs the attention of the reader. Use active verbs, and keep your headline short. Remember, a press release should be easy to understand and use without revision.

• The opening paragraph should summarize the details and answer the five basic questions mentioned in the first bulleted item of this list. You can add supporting paragraphs to provide more details, but the release should be written so that if the supporting paragraphs get cut, no critical information will be lost.

• If it's possible, include accurate quotes from people involved in your story. This will allow reporters to use the information without having to talk to the person.

• If you go to a second page, the word *More* should appear at the bottom center of the first page so that the reader knows there is more information. Type "###" at the bottom center of the last page, signaling to the reader the end of your release.

• The release should always be double spaced.

• Be sure to proofread and check your grammar. Read it aloud or ask someone to proofread it for you to make sure the information is simple, concise, and free of errors.

Ask, "Why is it important to have positive news about youth in our local papers, radio, and television reports?"

Step 1: Pass the newspaper clippings around (or ask youth to distribute the clippings they've collected) for youth to read. Ask if any in the group have submitted items like these for publication or broadcast. If so, ask these youth to explain how they did this, the challenges the encountered, and if their material was used. Tell the group what you have learned about how press releases and feature stories must be submitted to your local paper, radio station, or television station in order for them to consider using it. Review the press release template and tips (see below).

Step 2: As a group, identify positive youth activities that have taken place in the past week or will take place in the next month. Assign pairs to write a feature story or press release on the ones that they think are most newsworthy. Submit these for consideration, and follow up late to report on which were published or reported on radio or TV.

Sample Press Release

For Immediate Release   **Contact: [Name]**
[Date]   **Phone number:**

"Garage Theater" and Youth Actors Get Community Support

[Insert your city, state.]—A talented group of young people affectionately known as the "garage theater kids" have been putting on plays in one young actor's family garage for the past three years. The plays have been so well received that the actors need a real place to accommodate all the people who come to see their performances. This year the city has donated the use of its community center for the summer performance of *Without a Clue*, a Sherlock Holmes story.

   [Include more specific information and if possible, a quote such as the following: John Doe created this project six years ago and at 16 is still a major part of its success. "Whe I came up with this idea, I just wanted to give my friends a place to be creative," he says. "I didn't realize how many other teens were looking for something fun to do."

   [Your closing paragraph should contain follow-up information such as dates, times, and location.] The next two performances are at the City Community Center on Saturday, July 29, at 2:00 P.M. and 7:30 P.M. and Sunday, July 30, at 7:30 P.M.
                                                  ###
                          [This indicates the end of the press release.]

Service Coupons

Focus: Youth volunteer to help school staff members.

You will need:
index cards
markers
newsprint
tape (or an easel)

Set the stage: Recall for participants that school is where youth often learn about volunteer opportunities and also is where many students serve as volunteers. Ask youth to name volunteer opportunities they know of at school.

Step 1: Work as a group to list needs youth have observed in specific classrooms or other places in school that aren't "covered" by regular volunteer projects (for example, filing choir music, cleaning lab equipment, picking up litter in the parking lot, or decorating a hallway bulletin board). Ask each youth to choose one of these needs that he or she could give one hour of time per week to help meet. Think through supplies or materials that might be needed for these tasks and list them.

Step 2: Distribute index cards and markers for youth to use to prepare a "coupon" to present to a teacher or school staff person that is worth one hour of help with the specific need they selected. Encourage youth to report back on the response they received.

Step 3: Discuss the following:
• What was the reaction to your offer?
• How did it feel to step up and take the lead to get something going on a need you saw?
• Why are some volunteer jobs considered better than others?
• Was this activity satisfying or frustrating for you? Why?

Safety Improvement Project

Focus: Youth plan and implement a project to improve an unsafe situation in their community.

You will need:
clipboards
easel
markers
newsprint
pencils or pens
tape
writing paper

Step 1: Form teams of three. Ask each team to take a 10-minute walk around the building where you are meeting and, if practical, the immediate neighborhood. As they walk, they should look for safety hazards and write any they see on their clipboards. (Someone in each team should be wearing a watch to keep track of time.) Encourage youth to head in different directions to get different perspectives.

Step 2: When the group gathers again, have teams report on the safety hazards they noted. After each report, ask the group to decide which of the hazards reported is most dangerous and which hazard is most easily fixed. Record these on newsprint.

Step 3: Discuss the following:
• Which of the hazards could our group work to fix?
• Which of the hazards will need key leaders and/or organizations working together to address?
• Which hazards require the work of a professional (e.g., electrician, carpenter)?

Beyond the activity: Decide as a group which hazards your group will remedy and which the group wants to refer to others for action. Work together to create a list of tasks and a plan for the work and the referrals to take place. Set up a time line for when these actions will take place. Follow up in a later session to learn from each other what responses were received to the safety improvements completed and the referrals that were made.

What Makes a Good Leader?

Focus: Youth indicate leadership traits in youth and adult leaders they admire and in themselves.

Points to remember: After youth complete the worksheet, ask them to compare responses in pairs. Encourage discussion based on these questions:
• Which quality of a good leader is most important to you? Who is a good role model of this quality?
• Which leadership quality have you been able to demonstrate in your own life? How did you learn to do this?
• Which combination of qualities is most important for leaders who work with youth?

Passport to Safety

Focus: Youth identify the places they spend time and evaluate how safe and welcomed they are in those places.

Note: Some youth participants may not be familiar with a passport, so you may need to take a few minutes to explain. Bring your own passport in if you have one.

Points to remember: As a group, compare notes about where youth spent time during the past week. Make a list on newsprint of the places that are mentioned most often. Next, tally how many youth marked circles, stars, and/or hearts for each place on your list. Discuss:
• How many places did you mark with a combination of circle, star, and heart? Why do you think these places have a combination?
• What does this activity suggest about how you decide where to spend your time?
• Are there places where you have to spend time that have no heart, circle, or star? What can you do to be safer—physically and emotionally—in these places?

How Resource-Full Are You?

Focus: Youth identify the resources they bring to different areas of their lives.

Points to remember: Before youth complete the worksheet, ask, "Is it difficult to think of yourself as a resource to others? Why or why not?"

After youth complete the worksheet, allow time for each young person to share with the group one way in which he or she is a resource. As a group, talk about the following questions:
• How are your talents, skills, and attitudes different in the various places where you spend time? Why do you think that is so?
• Are there any places where you feel that you have resources to offer, but adults and other youth don't consider you as a resource? What could you do to change their perception of you?

How Are We Seen?

Focus: Youth observe how adults respond to youth who greet them.

Points to remember: Although this activity can be done individually, it may be more revealing and engaging if all youth in the group decide on a single action to try and then tally the results as a group. Introduce this activity asking: "In what ways do adults in our community view our youth? Why do you think there is a variety of reactions to young people?"

Think of ways youth can extend a friendly greeting to adults. Choose one that is appropriate for your community for the purpose of this activity, as described on the worksheet. After the group tallies its results, discuss the findings and how/if you should share what you observed with the community.

(For more ideas, see *Tag, You're It!,* a poster for youth and adults available from Search Institute.)

Discuss your findings as a group:

- What did you learn from this activity? How would you explain the results? (Encourage youth to consider that the responses they receive from some adults may be influenced by the expectations of their cultural background, age, or the kind of day they're having. Explore a little more to learn what different cultural groups consider as polite or respectful exchanges between individuals who are different ages and individuals who do not know each other.)

- If you repeated the action among the adults in your community for one full month, what do you think might happen? How about in six months?

- How do our initial contacts with individuals shape our opinion of them? Is this fair? Why or why not?

- What can youth do to help more adults consider them as responsible, contributing members of the community? What can adults do?

Beyond the activity: If youth are willing, challenge them to continue their experiment for several more weeks or months.

Think of a leader in your home, school, neighborhood, or community who has qualities you admire. What do you admire about that person? Write her or his name on the space provided below and write the qualities and skills that make the person a good leader inside the painting. Do you think of yourself as a leader? Why or why not?

NAME

Imagine that you've been traveling this past week and that you've collected a stamp on your passport for each place you've been. Write each place where you have spent time this past week inside one of the stamps. Circle each place where you felt safe. Put a star by each place where you felt welcome. Put a heart by each place where the adults and other youth have a positive relationship with you. If certain places have all three qualities, mark them accordingly with a circle, star, and heart. As you consider the past week, where do you wish you could spend more time? How can you improve the quality of places where you have to spend time?

Money is a resource that everyone recognizes. It's not always so easy to recognize how people can be resources, yet the gifts, talents, and attitudes that people bring can be much more valuable than money in the places we spend time each week. So, what kind of resource are you? Think about the talents, skills, and attitudes you bring or contribute to each of these places. Write them in the bills below. How can you give more of your resources—resources that are more valuable than money (e.g., time, energy, enthusiasm)?

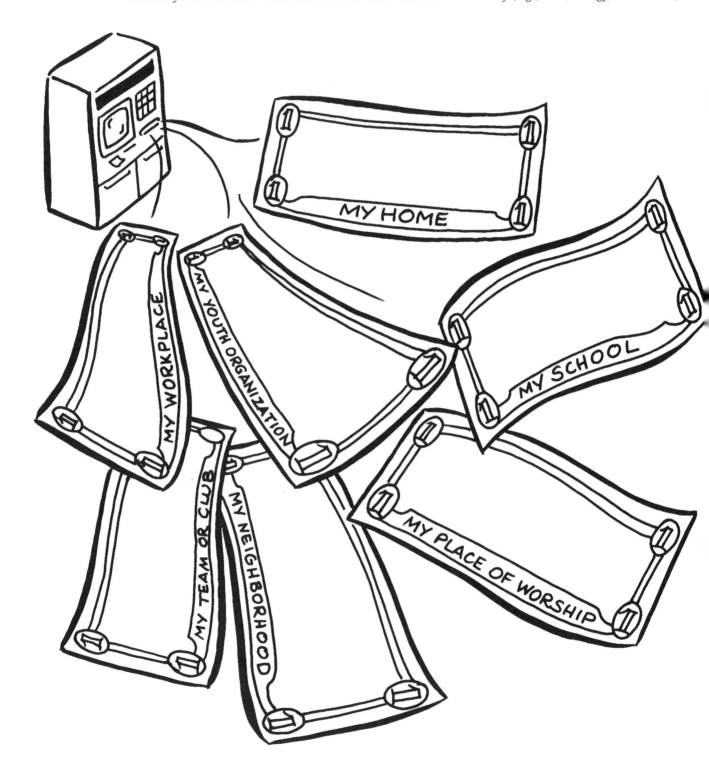

How do adults in your community respond when they meet you or other young people on the street or in a store? How do you respond to them? Try this activity to learn more about communication between youth and adults.

First, choose a greeting that you think most adults would perceive as a friendly gesture. You might look them in the eye and say "Hi" or smile and wave or nod. If you are part of a youth group, you may choose to use the same greeting and then compare results.

As you try out your greeting with adults you feel comfortable approaching, observe their responses to you, including their body language as well as anything that they say. Record your observations in the chart below.

Greeting we will use: _____

Observation record:

	Time	Place	Response from adult	Youth alone or with other youth?	Other observations
Adult 1					
Adult 2					
Adult 3					
Adult 4					
Adult 5					
Adult 6					
Adult 7					
Adult 8					

Summary of my observations: _____

_____

Why I think adults responded a certain way: _____

_____

_____

What do the results tell me about adults? _____

_____

_____

Chapter 4

The Boundaries-and-Expectations Assets

Young people need the positive influence of adults and peers who encourage them to be and do their best. They are more likely to thrive when they have clear rules about appropriate behavior, and consistent, reasonable consequences for breaking those rules. The activities in this chapter help youth better understand and appreciate the importance of these assets and encourage them to work with parents and others to strengthen these assets in their lives.

36 ── **How Old?**

Focus: Youth share information about family boundaries and their importance.

You will need:
• markers
• newsprint
• tape

Before the group arrives: Make signs that say 10, 12, 14, 16, 18, 21, and Don't Know. Post them around the room.

Set the stage: Point out the signs, saying that these are people's ages. Explain that as you read a list of activities many youth take part in, youth participants should go and stand by the sign that shows how old their parents or guardians, or other caring adults at home, say they must be in order to do that activity. If they don't know what the rule is for their family, they should stand by "Don't Know."

Step 1: After you read each activity, pause and ask if youth can share reasons why their parents have set the age boundary they have. Then ask for volunteers to share why they believe certain boundaries exist. Are these boundaries reasonable? Why or why not? Use this list of activities, changing items as necessary to better fit your community:

• Have a summer job
• Go to the mall without an adult
• Watch R-rated movies
• Buy a car
• Use the Internet without supervision
• Stay out until midnight
• Have a phone in your bedroom
• Open a checking account
• Get a credit card
• Go on a date
• Go out with a group of youth (without an adult)
• Do your own laundry
• Take a weekend trip with a friend's family
• Get a body part pierced
• Choose what clothes to buy
• Drink alcohol for the first time
• Have cell phone or pager
• Baby-sit for another family
• Stay home alone overnight
• Do chores around the house

Step 2: After youth have responded to all items, discuss:
• Why do different families have different age boundaries for the same activity?
• If you don't know what your family boundary is for a certain activity, how can you find out?
• How should a group of friends handle a situation in which some in the group are allowed to do a certain activity, but others aren't?
• How do the rules you have to follow compare to those that your siblings have to follow? Do your parents/guardians expect less of younger siblings? Why or why not?
• What can you do if you don't agree with a certain rule? (Ask participants to brainstorm positive solutions.)

37 ——————— Let's Play

Focus: Youth experience boundaries and expectations.

You will need:
- markers
- one pair of dice
- poster board
- very small toy cars (one per youth)

Before the group arrives: Make a game board by drawing a row of game spaces ("squares") around each of the four edges of the poster board. Make sure there are at least 48 spaces on the board (12 spaces per side). Mark one square as "Start." Label the rest of the squares at random: Move Ahead 2 Spaces; Go Back to Start; Lose Your Next Turn; Move Back 5 Spaces; Move Back 1 Space; Move Ahead 10 Spaces; Take Another Turn; Switch Places with Another Player. *(Note: If your group is large, make one game board for every eight youth.)*

Set the stage: As youth arrive, ask each one to choose a toy car to use as a game marker. Have them sit in a circle around the game board, and give the dice to one youth.

Step 1: Tell the group they have 10 minutes to play the game. Give no further instructions. Remain silent no matter how hard they beg!

Step 2: At the end of 10 minutes, stop play. Discuss:
- Who won? How did you know?
- What rules did the group seem to assume? Did these assumptions make the game easier or more difficult? Why do you think these assumptions were made?
- What rules did the group make as you went along? How did you decide what rules to use? Why did you make these rules?
- What happens when parents, teachers, or other leaders don't "tell you the rules" for what you are doing? What can you do when you find yourself in a situation where the rules or boundaries are not clear?

38 ——————— Creative Praise

Focus: Youth enlarge their vocabularies for offering praise and positive reinforcement to peers and younger children.

You will need:
- markers
- newsprint

Before the group arrives: A week or two before this activity, ask young people to record all the positive things they observe their friends or younger children doing or saying for one week.

Set the stage: Ask youth to name all the positive things they observed. Do this round-robin style; that is, each youth takes a turn to say one thing that he or she observed. If a young person cannot add a new example, he or she passes for that round. Keep going around the group until there are no more new examples.

Ask: "How many of these youth or children received some kind of response or recognition from others when they did or said something positive? What kinds of responses did they receive?"

Step 1: Form teams of three. Give each team a sheet of newsprint and a marker. Challenge them to brainstorm words and actions that would let others know their actions are appreciated and/or the right thing to do. After five minutes, ask each team to report back to the group.

Step 2: Then discuss:
- Is it important to praise or thank people when they do or say something that you appreciate or that you think is a good thing to do? Why or why not? Does it matter if the one doing the positive action is a child, a youth, or an adult?
- What kinds of responses are most meaningful to you? Which seem phony or routine?

- What kinds of responses do you think are most meaningful to young children?
- What kinds of responses do you think are most meaningful to adults?

39 ——————————— Climb That Mountain

Focus: Youth explore the relationship between expectations and boundaries.

You will need:
- bulletin board
- construction paper (assorted colors)
- markers
- tape

Set the stage: Ask youth to imagine an important goal in their lives as the top of a mountain. Getting to this goal is an expectation they have of themselves. Ask: "Is it important for close friends and family to agree with your goal and encourage your expectations? Why or why not?"

Step 1: Ask youth to imagine the road to the top of that steep mountain, full of curves, drop-offs, tempting detours that are dead ends, and streams to cross. One way to think about boundaries and rules is to imagine them as the guardrails and the warning signs that help a person stay on the road to the goal. Ask: "What are some boundaries and rules that close friends and family might put into place to help a young person reach her or his goal?"

Step 2: As a group, decide on a goal that is both common and desirable for youth in the community, such as graduating from high school. Tell the group that its task is to create a bulletin board display that will help other youth understand the boundaries and rules that will help them meet the expected goal. First, create a beautiful mountain and label the peak with the goal. Use markers to draw a winding road to the peak.

Step 3: Identify hazards along the way (e.g., working too many hours, drugs and partying, not doing homework, sexual activity/pregnancy, gambling, not taking care of your health, not getting enough sleep). Have youth decide how to depict these (e.g., streams, cliffs, dead-end roads), make these shapes out of construction paper, and label them. Tape in place along the mountain road.

Step 4: Now, invite youth to think about the boundaries that could help a young person stay on the road to this goal. Have youth decide how to depict these boundaries (guardrails, signs, bridges), make these shapes out of construction paper, and tape them to the mountain road.

Step 5: Finally, choose a name for the bulletin board and make the title with large construction paper letters (such as, We're Reaching New Heights!). Display the creation where everyone in the group can see it.

Step 6: Ask the following:
- What can a person learn when he or she is headed for a guardrail? What is the most helpful thing that friends or family members can do when this happens?
- How can a person make sure the journey is fun and not just a task or obstacle to overcome?
- Is it possible for the peak of the mountain to be too high? How would a person know if this were the case? What can be done if the goal and the expectations are unreasonable?

40 ────────── **It's a Rule**

Focus: Youth learn more about the boundaries in their school.

You will need:
- easel (or tape)
- markers
- newsprint
- self-stick note pads (6 sheets per youth)
- school handbooks, if available

Before the group arrives: Label three sheets of newsprint with "We Know the Rule," "There Ought to Be a Rule," and "This Rule Needs to Change." Post these around the room.

Step 1: Give each youth three self-stick notes. Ask youth to think of three rules in their school that they think are very clear. Tell them to write one of these rules on each note. As they finish, they can post these on the chart labeled "We Know the Rule."

Step 2: Ask youth to think of three areas of school life where they think a rule is needed, but where they don't think one exists. Tell them to write each of these situations on a self-stick note and post them on the chart labeled "There Ought to Be a Rule."

Step 3: As a group, look at the self-stick notes on both charts. First, determine if there are any notes on the "Ought" chart that have a corresponding rule on the "Know" chart. Talk about why young people may not have realized that a rule existed, asking such questions as, "Are young people as informed as they should be?"

Step 4: Next, if the school(s) that your youth attend have handbooks, distribute them and ask pairs to look for rules that may already exist for notes on the "Ought" chart. Discuss:
- What rules did you discover for some of these situations on the "Ought" chart? Why do you think these rules are not well known or not well enforced? What could you do to improve this situation?
- If a rule or boundary does not exist for an area of school life that needs one, what is the process for making a change? Challenge youth to investigate with school leaders the process for creating policies, rules, and boundaries.
- How is the climate of a school affected when there are many situations and areas on the "Ought" chart?
- How is the climate of a school affected when there is a clear list on the "Know" chart, but the enforcement of the rules and boundaries is not consistent or fair? What can youth do to improve this situation?

Variation: As a third category, ask youth to look for rules in the school handbook that are outdated or unfair and need to be changed. Ask them to write these situations on three self-stick notes and post them on the chart labeled "This Rule Needs to Change."

41 ────────── **Powers of Persuasion**

Focus: Youth experiment with peer influence and its effect on decision making.

You will need:
- inflated balloons
- index cards
- masking tape
- old newspapers
- small treats

Before the group arrives: Write each of these instructions on a separate index card. Each youth will need one card, so repeat some of them if necessary:
- Convince a person on your team to pop a balloon.
- Convince a person on another team to give you that team's tape.
- Convince a person on your team to work faster.
- Convince a person on your team to quit.
- Convince your team to use materials in addition to the ones provided.
- Convince a person on your team to rip a newspaper into shreds.
- Convince a person on your team to cheer on your team.
- Convince a person on your team to "trash talk" another team.

Set the stage: Distribute index cards to the group, instructing them to read the card silently and then put it inside a pocket or some other place where others cannot read it. Tell youth that during the game, they each are to do what is on the card, and to keep mental notes of how successful or unsuccessful they are. Suggest that they be subtle about what their "role" is so that others won't catch on too quickly.

Step 1: Form teams of four. Tell each team that its challenge is to build a structure that is at least 12 inches tall and will support two inflated balloons. Each team that can accomplish this within five minutes will get a reward. The first team that can accomplish this is the winner. Give each team a stack of old newspapers, a roll of masking tape, and two inflated balloons. Give a start signal and stand back.

Step 2: Call time after five minutes. Award a treats to teams who completed the task on time and applaud the winners. Gather as a group and ask each youth to report on her or his index card task. Ask each one:

- How well did your team work together? Why?
- Were you able to do what was instructed on the index card? What did you do to try to persuade another person? Was this easy or challenging for you? Why?

After all have reported, discuss:

- How do friends influence each other?
- Did you feel pressure to do what the others in your group were suggesting?
- What factors influence your decision about whether or not to be persuaded?

42 ──────────── **Neighborhood Charades**

Focus: Youth play a game to identify ways to be a responsible neighbor.

You will need:
- index cards
- markers
- newsprint
- small treats

Before the group arrives: Write each of these actions on a separate index card:

- Drive carefully.
- Know each other's names.
- Smile and wave to each other.
- Take care of your own property.
- Stop to chat once in a while.
- Respect the property of others.
- Tell children when they are doing something wrong.
- Tell children when they are doing something right.
- Help each other with chores.
- Watch a neighbor's home while the neighbor is on a trip.
- Fix safety hazards.
- Help in an emergency.

Step 1: Form teams of four, then tell each team to divide into two pairs. Tell the group that you are going to play "Charades" and that all of the answers will be things that good neighbors do. Ask youth to help you review some of the common hand signals used when playing "Charades." (You may also need to review the rules if youth aren't familiar with the game.)

Step 2: Choose the team wearing the most colors (shirts, shoes, socks) to start. Give an index card to one of the pairs. This pair has 30 seconds to prepare and then act out the action without words so that the other pair on their team can guess what it is. If the nonacting pair can guess the action within two minutes, the team gets one point. Continue the play with another team, and play until all the cards are used.

Step 3: Award a treat and a round of applause to the winning team. Then discuss:
- Which of these actions have you seen your own neighbors do? (Invite a few youth to tell about what happened in these cases.)
- What are the advantages of having neighbors who are caring and responsible? Are there any disadvantages? Why or why not?
- What can you do when the boundaries and rules that a neighbor thinks are important are different from what your family thinks are important?

43 — When I Was Your Age

Focus: Youth discuss how family boundaries have changed over the years.

Set the stage: Gather in a circle. Ask each youth to think of things that they have heard paren or other older relatives say that begin, "When I was your age . . ." After a moment, go around the circle, with each young person completing this sentence with something they have heard. Keep going around the circle until there are no more sayings. Discuss:
- Why do you think older relatives like to tell you, "When I was your age . . ."?
- What boundaries and rules seem to be the same for you as for your parents or other relatives when they were young? Which ones seem to be different?
- Why do some boundaries change from one generation to the next? Why do some stay the same Do you think your parents or other relatives would answer this question in the same way?

Beyond the activity: Gather responses from parents or other relatives to these questions. (Be sure to restructure the questions so that they are specifically for parents/guardians.) Possible options for collecting this information include: inviting adults to join your group at a future da assigning pairs of youth to do quick phone interviews during the time of this activity and repo back to the group; or asking youth to interview parents/guardians at home and report back later. When you have responses from the adults, ask youth:
- What surprised you in the responses from the adults?
- What boundaries and rules do you imagine you will set when you are the adult?

44 — Favorite Sayings

Focus: Youth gather motivational sayings from others.

You will need:
- markers
- paper
- pencils
- phones
- poster board

Before the group arrives: Cut poster board into sizes that will fit inside the door of a locker the school your youth attend.

Set the stage: As you begin this session, share some of your favorite motivational sayings, bringing in posters, plaques, or fridge magnets to show the group. Tell why these are meaningful to you.

Step 1: Give youth paper and pencils and send them out in pairs to search for motivational sayings. They should inspect hallways, bulletin boards, classroom and meeting room walls, desktops, and office doors and walls, listing all the motivational sayings they can find. They a could phone parents, teachers, friends, and other adults they know and ask them for their favorite sayings, verses, or slogans. Allow about 15 minutes for the search.

Step 2: When the pairs return, ask them to present three of their favorites to the group. Provide poster board pieces and markers for youth to use to make locker posters with one favorite saying.

Step 3: As youth are working, discuss:
- What makes a saying motivational for you?
- Where could a person look for more motivational sayings?
- Do you have a favorite motivational saying?
- Why do you think slogans and sayings help people?

Variation: Suggest that youth give their posters to a friend or family member as a gift.

45 ──────────── **Dear Dr. Friend**

Focus: Youth respond to issues that may arise when they support the boundaries of their friends.

You will need:
- markers
- newsprint
- tape

Before the group arrives: Write each of these three letters on a separate sheet of newsprint:
- Dear Dr. Friend: Four of us have been planning a weekend camping trip for a month. Now Don's dad says he can't go because there won't be an adult there. What do we do?
- Dear Dr. Friend: Kim's parents expect her to get high marks. She is totally stressed about homework. She never has time to go to the mall with us anymore. How can we get our friend back?
- Dear Dr. Friend: I know that Sam's smoking marijuana. I know that it would cause a war if Sam's parents knew. I'm afraid that Sam is getting hooked. Should I tell?

Set the stage: As you begin this activity, ask youth: "Where and when did you learn how to work out difficult situations with your friends?"

Ask youth to line up in alphabetical order, according to the first letter of their first name. Begin at one end of the line and form three teams. Tell each team that they are going to try their skill at being an advice columnist.

Step 1: Give each team one of the three letters. Ask them to pretend they are Dr. Friend and write a response on the newsprint.

Step 2: After four minutes, rotate the sheets so that each team gets a different letter. Teams should read what the first team wrote, then add any advice they have. After four minutes, rotate the sheets a final time and repeat the process.

Step 3: As a group, post all the letters on a wall and look at the advice given for each situation. Discuss:
- Which advice will yield the most positive outcome? Which advice will lead to more problems?
- Do friends have a responsibility to honor the boundaries set by the families of their friends? Why or why not?
- What role do friends play in helping each other live within the boundaries set by their families?
- What course of action makes the most sense when a group of friends is struggling with boundaries they don't all share?

Television Tally

Focus: Youth evaluate how television programming supports and/or undermines boundaries and expectations that are important to them.

Note: This activity may take extra time to coordinate.

Before the group arrives: Label one piece of newsprint "Important Boundaries" and the other "Important Expectations." Post these in your meeting space, some distance from each other.

Set the stage: Ask youth to think quietly for a moment about the rules or boundaries that are most important to them, their families, and their school. Then ask them to think for a moment about the expectations they have for themselves and that their families and schools have for them that are most important. Allow a few minutes for youth to choose markers and write two or three responses on each of the charts.

Step 1: After all have written on the charts, give each youth five dots to mark the items on the list that he or she thinks are most important. Tally and make a chart of the top three boundaries and the top three expectations.

Step 2: Ask youth to pair up and watch network television for at least one hour (time may vary), keeping track of how many times they observe something that supports or undermines these top boundaries and expectations. Ask pairs to write down examples of the strongest support and the strongest undermining thing they see or hear.

Step 3: After pairs compare notes with each other, discuss:
- Who did a better job of upholding the boundaries and expectations—the ads or the shows? Why do you think this was the case?
- Does it matter if the television programming you watch supports or undermines the boundaries and expectations that are important to you, your family, and your school? Why or why not? Would your answer be different if I had asked about the programming that five-year-olds watch? Why or why not?
- If you watched the same network for one week, do you think the results of your observations would be the same? Why or why not?
- What boundaries and expectations do you set for yourself regarding television viewing? How about your families and your school?
- Does time of day have anything to do with how programming may differ?

Variation: If you have access to only one television, ask half the group to watch for strongest support messages and the other half to watch for the strongest undermining messages (as described above).

You will need:
- dot labels (self-adhesive "sticky dots")
- markers
- newsprint
- several televisions for viewing network programming

Changing the Boundaries

Focus: Youth consider positive ways to work with others to change boundaries

Points to remember: After youth complete the worksheet, ask youth to share examples of when they tried one of the suggestions on the sheet and what happened when they did. Discuss:

- What suggestions would you add to this list?
- What criteria would you use to help you think about whether a boundary should be changed or not?
- When would it make the most sense to work as an individual to change a boundary? When would it be a better idea to work with a group of youth?
- If you were to create a list of tips for adults, would it contain the same items? Why or why not?

Portrait of a Role Model

Focus: Youth highlight positive traits in an adult they admire.

Points to remember: As youth complete this worksheet, form a group list of positive traits of role models. Ask:

- Are these traits ones that American culture celebrates or rewards? Why do you think that is?
- What are the advantages of having role models? What are the disadvantages?
- Do celebrities make good role models? Why or why not?
- Can a young person be a role model for another young person? Why or why not?

What's Your Friend Potential?

Focus: Youth consider their qualities that contribute to building positive peer relationships.

Points to remember: This worksheet is primarily an opportunity for youth to reflect on their own skills in making and keeping friends. Be careful not to press youth to reveal information that they want to keep to themselves.

Discussion could include questions like:

- What else would you add to this list?
- How do people learn how to be a friend?
- What are the most important lessons you've learned about being a good friend?
- What advice would you give a young person who wants to have more friends?

Expectations

Focus: Youth identify expectations that influence their behavior.

Points to remember: Encourage youth to complete this individually. Share information in pairs. Discuss some of these questions:

- Which parts of the chart were easiest to complete? Which were more difficult?
- Are any of these expectations more important than others? Why or why not?
- If you were unable to fill in a box on the chart, how could you find out what those expectations are?

Boundaries and Children

Focus: Youth consider effective strategies for enforcing boundaries with younger children.

Points to remember: Invite youth who know children of these ages to add characteristics about them on this worksheet. During this discussion you might share some of the following features that have been determined about younger children:

Three-year-old: eye-hand coordination still developing—expect spills; does pretty well feeding and dressing self; rapidly increasing vocabulary—may repeat words without knowing the meaning; hungry for approval from adults and older youth; curious—asks lots of questions; prefers simple routines with limited choices; very active; wants to help.

Six-year-old: large muscles more developed than small ones; very active, but can sit still for six or eight minutes; may struggle when making decisions; likes to dramatize; beginning to understand need for appropriate manners and behavior; eager for responsibility.

Nine-year-old: strong sense of right and wrong; concerned about fairness; likes to spend time with group of same-sex friends; loves to talk—learning how to argue; likes to collect things; developing individual interests; can be a perfectionist; interested in other countries; loyal to own country.

Ask them to give examples "from real life" that illustrate the features. Discuss:
- Have you ever observed a parent/guardian, teacher, or older youth enforcing a rule with a three-year-old? What strategies were used? What seemed to be effective?
- Do you remember how parents, teachers, and older youth helped you understand and honor boundaries when you were six years old? When you were nine years old? What did they do? How did you feel about it?
- When is it appropriate for you to enforce a boundary with a younger child? When would it be inappropriate for you to do so?

Top 10 Expectations of Friends

Focus: Youth reflect on the importance of positive peer expectations.

Points to remember: If your group prefers cooperative projects, form teams of three to complete these lists. Allow time for each youth or small team to share the list they created and explain why they chose each item. Discuss:
- What can friends do or say to hold each other to high standards?
- What are the advantages of having friends with high expectations for themselves and others? Are there any disadvantages?
- What characteristics or traits do you admire in a friend?

Have you ever felt like a boundary or rule was unfair or inappropriate for your age? What did you do? Here are some ideas to try when you—either alone or with others—are working with a parent/guardian, teacher, or other adult leader to change a boundary. Which strategies will work for you? Rank these ideas from most effective to least effective. Give 1 to the idea that you think would work the best for you and 8 to the idea that you think is the least likely to work for you. Rank the others from 2 to 7.

 Think through your reasons for changing the boundary. Be prepared to present your ideas.

 Set a time when everyone involved will be able to focus on the conversation (not in a hurry, not tired, not hungry).

Call for a "time-out" if the conversation gets too heated. Pick it up again at a later time.

 Ask questions so that you understand the reasons for the boundary.

 Ask a "neutral third party" (such as a youth leader or counselor) to act as the moderator, making sure everyone gets a turn to speak and that the conversation stays positive.

 Have options to offer for how the boundary could be changed, and what the new consequences might be for violating the boundary.

 Listen carefully to what others say during the conversation and maintain eye contact with them.

Whatever the result, thank the others in the conversation for taking the time to talk with you about the boundary.

Which adults do you admire? Choose one of these adults and write her or his name on the line. As you think about this person, answer the questions in the conversation bubbles (as you think he or she would answer them). Then think about what you have learned from watching this person. Which of the qualities you noted in the bubbles do you feel *you* have?

ONE ADULT I ADMIRE IS: _____

HOW DO I VIEW THE WORLD?

WHAT GREAT THINGS DO I SAY? WHAT WORDS DO I USE OFTEN?

HOW DO I TREAT OTHER PEOPLE?

WHAT WORTHWHILE THINGS DO I DO?

HOW DO I PUT MY BELIEFS INTO ACTION?

ROLE-MODEL QUALITIES I SEE IN MYSELF:

Do you make new friends easily? Do you feel you do a good job of keeping friends? This sheet has a list of skills and characteristics that help you make and keep friends. Take a few minutes to rate yourself on each one. When you're done, choose one or two skills you want to work on improving this month. Remember, you can help your friends build asset #15, positive peer influence, by being a great friend.

listen as much as I talk when I'm with my friends.

| Hardly ever | Some of the time | Most of the time |

suggest things to do that other people think are fun.

| Hardly ever | Some of the time | Most of the time |

refuse to repeat gossip or hurtful comments about others.

| Hardly ever | Some of the time | Most of the time |

an sense when my friends are angry, frustrated, or feeling left out—even if they don't say anything.

| Hardly ever | Some of the time | Most of the time |

tand up for what I think is right, even if my ends do not agree.

| Hardly ever | Some of the time | Most of the time |

an tell a joke.

| Hardly ever | Some of the time | Most of the time |

pologize when I goof up.

| Hardly ever | Some of the time | Most of the time |

"random acts of kindness" for friends and others.

| Hardly ever | Some of the time | Most of the time |

I keep the promises I make.

| Hardly ever | Some of the time | Most of the time |

I can disagree with someone without getting angry or resorting to name-calling.

| Hardly ever | Some of the time | Most of the time |

I keep secrets.

| Hardly ever | Some of the time | Most of the time |

I encourage friends to do their best.

| Hardly ever | Some of the time | Most of the time |

I forgive others who ask for forgiveness.

| Hardly ever | Some of the time | Most of the time |

I work to mend my relationship with a friend after an argument.

| Hardly ever | Some of the time | Most of the time |

I join in celebrating when a friend succeeds.

| Hardly ever | Some of the time | Most of the time |

I reach out to people who seem lonely or disconnected.

| Hardly ever | Some of the time | Most of the time |

50 Expectations

Do you know what is expected of you? Do you know what others expect you to do and how they expect you to do it? Is enough expected of you—or too much? Think about these questions as you fill in the chart below. Where the expectations aren't clear or aren't at a comfortable level, talk about them with the people mentioned.

	What I expect of myself	What my family expects of me	What my teachers expect of me	What my friends expect of me
Personal values that should guide the decisions I make				
Taking care of my own health and safety				
Appropriate behavior				
How I treat others				
What my future should be				
Other expectations				

Boundaries and Children

Sometimes younger children need to be reminded about what's right and wrong. As an older person in their lives, you can help your younger siblings, relatives, or friends make the right choices.

Read the three situations below and write some of the things you would say or do to a child at age three, six, or nine. Compare your notes with the others in your group to learn more ideas about working with younger children.

3-year-old

You spot her or him running into the street to get a ball.

My response:

6-year-old

He has wandered away from home to a neighbor's house, without telling anyone. It takes you 20 minutes to find him.

My response:

9-year-old

You pick her up from school and you see her making fun of another child.

My response:

Your parents have expectations for what you should do and how. So do your teachers and other adult leaders. What about your friends? What do they expect of you? What do you expect of them? Is it "the best"? Create a list here of your top ten expectations of your friends. How can you encourage your friends to be and do their best?

TOP 10 EXPECTATIONS

1. _____
2. _____
3. _____
4. _____
5. _____
6. _____
7. _____
8. _____
9. _____
10. _____

I CAN ENCOURAGE MY FRIENDS TO BE AND DO THEIR BEST BY: _____

Chapter 5

The Constructive-Use-of-Time Assets

Young people need opportunities outside of school to learn and develop new skills and interests, and to spend enjoyable time interacting with other youth and adults. The activities in this chapter encourage youth to get involved in building these assets.

53 — Ask Dr. Time

Focus: Youth offer advice in scenarios regarding time-use issues in families.

You will need:
- markers
- newsprint

Before the group arrives: Write each of these letters on separate sheets of newsprint:
- Dear Dr. Time: I made the basketball team, and now I have a lot of practices and games. My parents/guardians still expect me to do chores at home. There's no time! What can I do?
- Dear Dr. Time: I love to play cards with my family. No one ever has time for a game anymore. What can we do?
- Dear Dr. Time: I have a big family. I feel like I never get any time to spend by myself because someone's always around. I end up leaving home for peace and quiet. What can I do?

Step 1: Form three teams. Give each team one of the letters and ask them to think of how they would respond to the writer. After about five minutes, ask each team to plan a short skit that shows "Before" and "After"—the problem and the solution suggested by Dr. Time.

Step 2: After each team has presented its skit, ask:
- Why do families have conflicts regarding time?
- What advice would you give to a family to help it manage the limited resource of time?
- What is the most challenging part of getting through everything you have to do in one day? What is the most challenging part of coordinating your schedule with your family's schedule?

54 — Time Jars

Focus: Youth assemble time jars to experience time management principles.

You will need:

Gather for each pair of youth:
- crayons (or markers)
- five smaller rocks that will fit in jar along with the three big rocks
- gravel (one cup) in a sandwich bag
- newsprint
- one glass or plastic pint jar (no lid needed)
- sand (one cup) in a sandwich bag
- three large rocks that will all fit in the jar at the same time

Before the group arrives: Print or write each of the eight asset categories on a separate sheet of paper and post them around the room for participants to refer to during the activity. (Or write the eight categories on a blackboard or dry-erase board where everyone can see them.)

Step 1: Ask youth to work in pairs. Give each pair a crayon and a sheet of newsprint to work on, then distribute the jars, rocks, gravel, and sand. Tell youth that the jars represent the amount of time they have in one Wednesday, and the rocks and sand represent things they need or want to do on that Wednesday.

Step 2: Have youth think about Wednesday next week and decide what the big rocks might be that day—the things that are absolutely essential for them to do. Tell them to write these on their newsprint with crayons.

Step 3: Ask youth to think about what the small rocks would be next Wednesday—the things that are fairly important to do. Tell them to write these on the newsprint as well. Have them think about what things need to be done but wouldn't have to be done on Wednesday. These things are the gravel. Tell them to write three of these things on the newsprint. Finally, have them think about what things they would like to do if they have time next Wednesday—the sand. They should write three of these things on the newsprint.

Step 4: Encourage youth to organize their ideas using the eight asset categories that are posted around the room. Ask pairs to tell the group some of the things they have written on their newsprint.

Step 5: Comment that all of us have things we really like to do, so they should pour their sand into their jars first. Now tell them to add the rest of their rocks and gravel. What happens? Challenge youth to figure out how to make it all fit into the jar. (If youth have trouble figuring out how to do this, suggest that they put the big rocks in first.)

Step 6: After pairs complete their time jars, discuss:
• What did you learn about planning from this activity?
• What would your big rocks be if you were doing a time jar for an entire week? Why are they the same or different?
• What would your big rocks be for a day during school vacation?

55 — Organization Share Fair

Focus: Youth describe the organizations to which they belong.

Note: This activity will take more than one session.

Before the group arrives: Make a list on newsprint of all the organizations, clubs, or teams to which your youth belong.

Set the stage: Suggest that group members should have an opportunity to tell each other about their organizations—what they do, why it's good to be a member, and how to become a member. Plan an Organization Share Fair for an upcoming session. Decide if you should invite friends or younger youth to join you for this session.

Step 1: Ask each youth to decide which organization he or she wants to present. If more than one young person belongs to a given organization, a pair could present a single organization. Note on the newsprint which youth will prepare information about which organization.

Step 2: Encourage youth to bring materials about their organizations. They also should make chart that describes the top three benefits of being a member, as well as how to become a member. During the fair, have youth take turns staying with their display and visiting other displays.

Step 3: Ask the group the following:
• What is the best way to invite another person to join your organization?
• Do you think it's easier for youth to be involved in school, community, or religious activities? Wh
• Which activities in your community and school seem to attract the most youth? What reasons ca you think of for their popularity?
• How often are new people welcome to join?

Variation: For youth who aren't part of an organization, ask them to write down some of the interests on a sheet of paper. During the discussion encourage these youth to ask questions a find out more about various community organizations from their peers. Help them contact su organizations (by providing contact names and phone numbers, etc.).

You will need:
• easels for displaying items
• markers
• newsprint
• pencils or pens
• tables
• writing paper

Focus: Youth present questions about youth activities to religious institutions (e.g., mosques, temples, churches, synagogues).

Note: This activity will take more than one session.

Set the stage: Ask youth how many took part in an activity at a religious institution during the past month. Take a few minutes for youth to describe what they did. Ask:
- What opportunities do you have in your religious organization that you can't get in other places?
- When you are taking part in religious activities, are you usually with people of all ages or mostly with other young people? What are the advantages and disadvantages of this? For example, can anyone come, or just members?

You will need:
- information booklets for your community
- markers
- newsprint
- Yellow Pages

Step 1: Ask pairs of youth to search the Yellow Pages and any community information you brought and make a list of five religious institutions in their community. If youth have difficulty narrowing down their choices, encourage them to pick the religious institutions that appear the most interesting or those that advertise youth programs.

Step 2: Find out what questions youth have about opportunities for young people in these institutions. Note them on newsprint. Decide on three or four questions that you will ask each institution.

Step 3: Have volunteers sign up for the religious institution they would like to contact. Encourage them to send e-mail messages with their questions or plan to phone a youth leader.

Step 4: After youth have the information, decide how it could be shared with other young people. Perhaps it could be posted on a community Web site or put in a newsletter for youth.

7 ——————————— **Is It a Waste of Time?**

Focus: Youth examine the ways they spend their time.

You will need:
- copier paper in several colors (waste paper printed on one side works fine)
- markers
- recycling container (might also use a trash can or large box)
- small treat

Step 1: Form teams of three or four youth. Assign each team a different color and give it a stack of copier paper in its color and markers. Challenge each team to think of 10 ways that people waste time. Teams should write each way on a different sheet of paper. Ask them to choose their three favorite ways.

Step 2: Ask each team to read its three favorite ways to waste time to the group. Ask for a show of hands to indicate which youth consider themselves "guilty" of wasting time in each way as it is read.

Step 3: Place the recycling container about 10 feet behind a line that you indicate with tape or some other mark on the floor. Tell teams to wad their papers into balls and see how many they can throw into the container within two minutes. Paper wads that miss can be retrieved, but all must be thrown from behind the line. Award a small treat to the team that gets the most paper wads into the container.

Step 4: As a group, discuss:
- Did your team agree on all the time wasters that were suggested by individual team members? Why or why not? Who decides what is a waste of time?
- Is "sitting and doing nothing" always a waste of time? Why or why not?
- When is it a good idea to pause and do nothing for a few minutes?

Give It a Try

Focus: Youth experiment with different art mediums.

Before the group arrives: Consult with a youth participant or teacher of young children and gather assorted art supplies commonly used by young children for art projects, especially supplies that are new on the market.

Set the stage: As youth arrive, invite them to look at the various art supplies and choose one that looks especially fun or interesting. Tell them to make something to give to another person. Be prepared to give ideas, such as a picture for the fridge at home, a card for a relative, a poster for a child, a bracelet for a friend, or a song or poem for a parent or guardian. If a holiday is approaching, you could suggest making items connected with that theme. Try playing relaxing music as participants work to help them concentrate.

Step 1: After 20 minutes, have a short time of "show and tell," and then discuss:
• What was your first reaction to this activity—were you excited, dreading it, or indifferent?
• What worries did you have as you started?
• What did you learn as you made your project? How did you feel while you were working on it?
• Why are many people reluctant to try something new, especially something related to art? What advice would you give a friend who is hesitant to try a new creative activity?

Creative Circles

Focus: Youth play a game and discover ways to express their creativity.

Points to remember: You may choose to review the games instructions with the group before they begin. Remind youth that they can move their game pieces (coins) horizontally or diagonally as long as the space that they move to is connected to their previous space. After pairs have completed the game, ask the group:
• What are the benefits of expressing your creativity in art, writing, music, or drama?
• Where are you most comfortable exercising your creative side?
• How does our community support creativity in youth and adults?

Get Involved!

Focus: Youth help others discover the benefits of participating in youth programs.

Points to remember: If you are doing this activity in a group setting, spend a few minutes brainstorming words and short phrases that describe the benefits of participating in organized youth activities. Youth may prefer to work in pairs to create puzzles. After the puzzles are finished, you may want to photocopy them for use in newsletters or to give to classes of younger children.

Put It on Your PDA (Personal Digital Assistant)

Focus: Youth indicate how each of these four assets can be part of their week.

Points to remember: Before youth begin the worksheet, review with them the four Constructive-Use-of-Time assets. If you have information for your community from Search Institute's *Profiles of Student Life: Attitudes and Behaviors* survey, share the results for these four assets. Discuss:
• What is the most difficult thing about balancing the demands on your time?
• If you could add one hour to each day, what would you do with it?

The Place Where You Live

Focus: Youth assess how their time at home is spent.

Points to remember: Begin a discussion with questions like:
• What do you gain from the time you spend at home? (Be sensitive to youth who may be from homes where they are not safe and supported.)
• Are there any activities you marked as "alone" activities that you wish were done with others? Are there any activities you marked as "with others" that you would rather do alone? What could you do to influence a change?

When someone says it's time for a "creative activity," do you find a way to leave the room? Play this game to consider how creativity is part of your life and your community each day.

Directions: Use a coin as a game piece (one per youth). You also will need one die. After you roll the die, you can move to a circle with that number, but it must be connected with your current place by a line. When you land on a new circle, you must be able to name one place in your community where you can do the activity mentioned or else go back to your previous place. If there is no connecting circle with the number you roll, you lose your turn. First player to the top wins.

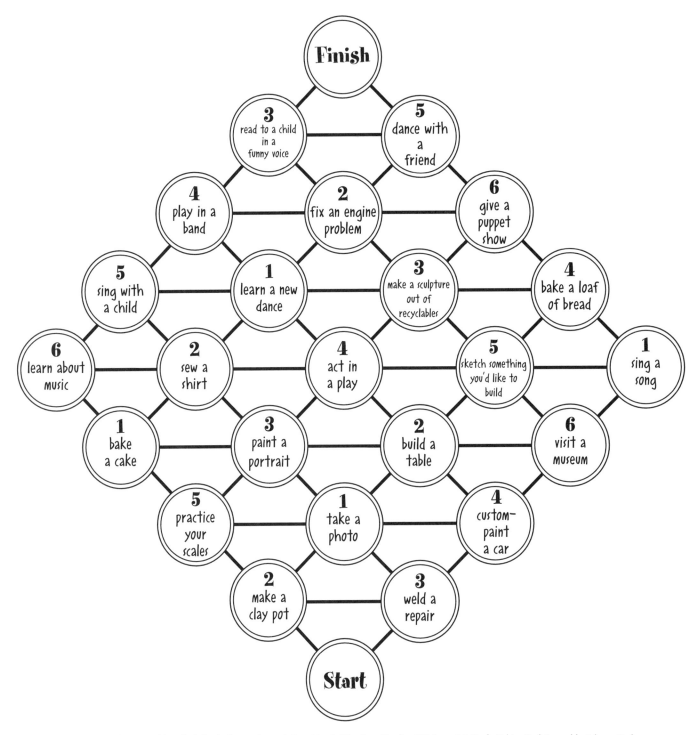

Imagine you are on the "member recruiting committee" for a youth organization or group. What words and phrases could you use to explain to other youth the benefits of joining this organization? Think of at least 10 words and write them on the lines under the puzzle. Create a word search puzzle that proclaims the benefits of belonging to a youth group or organization by writing your words and phrases on the grid forward, backward, vertically, or diagonally. Fill in the extra spaces with random letters. Trade puzzles with a friend and see who can solve it more quickly. Or, offer your puzzle to another group to solve. You also could publish a puzzle in your school, organization, or community newsletter.

Put In on Your PDA (Personal Digital Assistant)

The four Constructive-Use-of-Time assets are:

- **Creative activities—**Young person spends three or more hours per week in lessons or practice in music, theater, or other arts.
- **Youth programs—**Young person spends three or more hours per week in sports, clubs, or organizations at school and/or in the community.
- **Religious community—**Young person spends one or more hours per week in activities in a religious institution.
- **Time at home—**Young person is out with friends "with nothing special to do" two or fewer nights per week.

At what times during your week are you building these assets? Mark this calendar to show the days and times when you're involved in activities that build each of these assets.

The Place Where You Live

What do you do when you're at home? Jot down your at-home activities in the rooms of this playhouse. Now, use this code to mark each of your at-home activities:

✔ Activities that you do alone
➜ Activities that you do with people who are not related to you
♥ Activities that you do with your family

How do you feel about the balance of your at-home activities? What would you like to change?

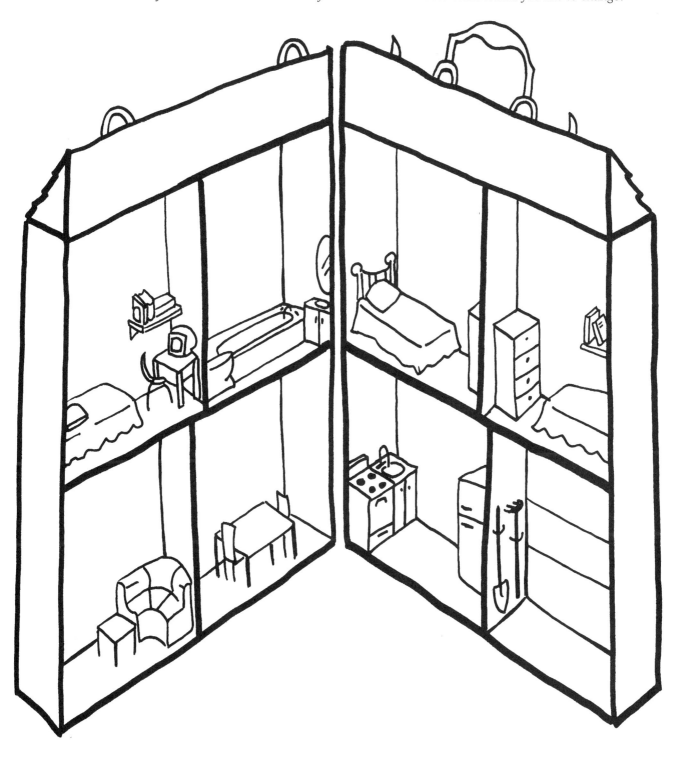

Chapter 6

The Commitment-to-Learning Assets

Young people need a positive attitude toward learning, including the desire for academic success, a sense of the lasting importance of learning, and a belief in their own abilities. Their sense of belonging to their school is an important ingredient in how they perceive the value of learning. The activities in this chapter will challenge youth to develop a commitment to learning and growing in both formal and informal ways.

63

Designer Book Covers

Focus: Youth create book covers that promote their schools.

You will need:
• markers
• newsprint (or brown grocery bags cut to the size of book covers)
• tape

Set the stage: As youth arrive, ask them to write the spirit slogans that their school(s) use in cheers, banners, and stickers. Challenge them to create some new ones that highlight their favorite, positive aspects of school(s), or encourage youth to create a motivational message that they think is more fitting for themselves and their circle of friends. To help youth develop their ideas, ask questions such as, "What's important to you and other students?" "What are the things you'd like to change about your school?" "What are the types of messages you'd like to hear (or others need to hear) when you are at school?"

Step 1: Have youth work in pairs to design book covers to use on their textbooks. Provide plenty of markers.
As youth are working, discuss:
• Why do schools have slogans?
• How do slogans affect students, teachers, and others (administrators, counselors, custodians) in the school? What affect do they have on people in the community?
• Can slogans make a difference in how students feel about their school? Why or why not?
• What positive messages would you convey that aren't reflected in the slogan?

Variation: Instead of a slogan, encourage youth to sketch a drawing or create a collage that expresses their positive feelings toward school, their friends, or staff members.

64

Learning through the Year

Focus: Youth exchange ideas about learning outside the school setting in their community.

Note: This project may take more than one session to complete.

You will need:
• large bulletin board
• markers
• newsprint
• yarn or construction paper strips

Before the group arrives: Cover a bulletin board with fresh paper and use yarn or construction paper strips to outline 12 squares. Label each with a month of the year.

Set the stage: Explain that youth will form teams by walking around the room and whispering the month of their birthday. As youth find others from the same month, they form a team. If your group is small, combine several months.

Step 1: Ask each team to begin a list of things to do during that month in their community that would promote individual learning outside of school (service projects, seasonal books to read, places to investigate, field trips, types of activities to enjoy). Teams should write these on the appropriate squares on the bulletin board. Invite them to add seasonal drawings as well.

Step 2: If you want more extensive lists, ask youth to research community and organization calendars, investigate community education offerings, and check for resources at the library.

Step 3: As the group reviews the work on the bulletin board, ask:

- Which of these activities have you done? What kinds of things have you learned by doing them?
- Which activities involve people of many different ages?
- Why do communities or organizations plan these kinds of events or projects?

65 — Where's the Common Ground?

Focus: Youth discover what members of their group have in common.

You will need:
- 40 Developmental Asset List (one per student)
- pencils or pens
- writing paper

Set the stage: First, form pairs of youth by lining up according to age, then pairing the first person in line with the last person in line, and so on. Ask the pairs to list everything they can that they have in common—from the mundane to the important. (If pairs are struggling to get started on this list, suggest comparing notes on things like favorite color, favorite ice cream, knowing how to swim.)

Step 1: After five minutes, have pairs form teams of four. Each pair reads their list to the team then the team looks for things on both lists. Teams create a new list of things that their team of four has in common, adding other items that they may discover.

Step 2: After four minutes, have teams of four join to form teams of eight. Each team of four reads its list to the new team, then the eight youth look for things that are in common on the two lists. Teams create a new list of things that their team of eight has in common, adding other items that they may discover.

Step 3: Finally, call the teams together and compare lists to compile a list of things that your entire group has in common. Then discuss:

- Is the list of what our group has in common longer or shorter than you would have expected? Why do you think that is?
- What items on this list surprise you? If you were to do this activity with your entire school, what items might be on the list?
- Would knowing about the things you have in common with other youth influence your feelings about your school? Why or why not?
- Is a sense of common ground important to you? Why or why not?
- How could the developmental assets framework become a starting point for common ground in a school?

66 —————————— ## What Shape Is Your School In?

Focus: Youth display their feelings about their school.

You will need:

- index cards
- pencils or pens
- two chenille stems (long, colorful "pipe cleaners" found in craft supply stores) per youth

Set the stage: Instruct the youth to ask themselves, "If I had to describe my school as a shape, an object, or an animal, what would it be?" Invite each youth to select two chenille stems to make the shape, object, or animal that describes what they think their school is like.

Step 1: Form teams of three. Ask youth to tell each other about the shapes they have made. Teams should then combine all their chenille stems to make a sculpture that describes what they would like their school to be more like. Give each team an index card and pencil or pen to use for adding a title to their sculpture.

Step 2: As teams show their sculptures to the group, ask them to interpret the shapes, relating the ideas that they discussed for what they would like their school to be.

Step 3: Focus your discussion by asking:

- What makes youth feel connected to their school? What makes youth feel disconnected from their school?
- Why do some youth care about their school and others do not?
- What needs to happen so that a student who doesn't care much about her or his school begins to care more about it?
- How can a school community reach out to youth who feel isolated or disconnected? What role do students have? What role do teachers have? Parents and guardians?

Variation: Instead of chenille stems you might try children's modeling clay.

67 —————————— ## Book Poster

Focus: Youth create posters to encourage children to read.

You will need:

- an assortment of children's picture books (ask a librarian for suggestions) markers
- newspaper ads for current movies poster board cut in fourths (one piece per pair of youth)

Set the stage: As youth arrive, ask each one to choose a picture book. Form pairs of youth whose book covers have at least one matching color.

Step 1: Have youth read their selected books aloud to each other. As they finish reading, ask them to list three things about each book that they think would appeal to a young child.

Step 2: In the group, pass around the movie ads and ask:

- How do movie advertisers try to convince you to go to their movie? What kinds of words and images do they typically use? Are these words and images positive or negative?
- What positive words and images could you use to convince young children to read the books you just read?
- Why do we want to encourage young children to read books like these?

Step 3: Have each pair design posters to promote the books they read. Challenge them to use the same techniques they observe in movie advertising to convince young readers to look at the book. Remind them to use language young children will understand and be able to read.

Beyond the activity: After admiring the posters, give them to a child-care facility, the library, or a teacher in the primary grades.

68

Stick to Your School

Focus: Youth name positive aspects of their school.

You will need:
- bowl of pretzel sticks
- napkins

Set the stage: Gather in a circle. Pass the napkins and the bowl of pretzels around the circle. Invite each youth to take some pretzels, but to not eat them yet.

Step 1: Explain that when it's their turn, youth must say one good or positive thing about their school for each pretzel stick they have taken. After youth have made their remarks, they can eat the pretzels.

Step 2: While the group is munching, discuss:
- When you hear other youth talking about your school, are most comments negative or positive? Why do you think this is the case? Are staff and teachers setting the example for students?
- Do conversations among youth about school (classes, teachers, administrators, coaches, the building, and so on) shape their attitudes about school? Why or why not? If you have time, form two teams and talk about this.
- What can you do when you are part of a conversation that you think is too negative?
- What needs to happen in order for attitudes to change?

69

Dream Teacher

Focus: Youth describe qualities of effective teachers.

You will need:
- markers
- scissors
- sheets of paper (butcher paper, newsprint, bulletin board paper) at least 36 inches wide and 5 feet long—one sheet per three participants and several extra sheets
- tape

Set the stage: Begin the activity by commenting that participants have known a lot of teachers and are authorities on what makes a great teacher. Ask the group to brainstorm a list of characteristics, skills, and traits that make a person an effective and caring teacher. List these as they are mentioned. Probe this list by asking youth to give examples of these qualities in teachers they have known.

Step 1: Form teams of three, telling teams that their assignment is to create a "dream teacher." Have each team trace the outline of one team member on the paper and cut it out. As youth add details to their "person" with markers, challenge them to be creative in illustrating as many of the qualities of a good teacher as they can (for example, big, heart-shaped ears for being a caring listener, eyes in the back of the head for attentiveness, funny hat for sense of humor, and so on). Post the cutouts around the room.

Step 2: After the group has admired each team's work, discuss:
- How likely is it that one person could have most of these qualities?
- Which of these characteristics do you possess? Which of these characteristics do you observe in other youth in our group?
- At what times in your life do *you* have the opportunity to be a caring and effective teacher for someone?

Plan to display the outlines in a teachers' lounge or where classes of teachers are in training.

70 ———————————— **Library Scavenger Hunt**

Focus: Youth explore the available resources in their school or community library.

You will need:
- photocopies of scavenger hunt list
- small treats

Before the group arrives: Work with a librarian in your local library or school to create a scavenger hunt list that highlights the different kinds of materials available for recreational or pleasure reading. Items may include an article about a current popular musician; a book on a hobby you'd like to have; a review of a current movie; a book that will help you cook dinner in your first apartment; a list of things to do in Yellowstone National Park; something scary; something to help you get along better with your boss; something funny; something from a newspaper in a different state; or ideas for how to invest your money.

Also plan a time for the scavenger hunt and tell youth to bring their library cards or identification (such as a school ID) that will allow them to sign up for one (check with the librarian to find out what is required to obtain a library card).

Step 1: Meet at the library for this session or walk there as a group from your usual meeting space.

Step 2: Form teams of three by lining up in alphabetical order by street name; then starting at one end of the line, count off to form teams of three. Remind teams to honor the rules of the library (staying quiet, etc.) as they locate the scavenger hunt items and either check out, photocopy, or print out everything on the list.

Step 3: Award first and second prizes to the first two teams that finish, and other awards to each remaining team, such as the "Slow but Sure" team or the "Lost in the Shelves" team.

Step 4: Invite the librarian to join your discussion about items that were discovered, and thank her or him for helping with this activity. Ask the librarian to talk about why he or she thinks it's a good use of time to read for pleasure and to answer questions from the group. Also, allow time for youth who do not have library cards to apply for them.

71 ———————————— **Homework Helpers**

Focus: Youth share helpful tips for doing homework.

You will need:
- pencils or pens
- writing paper

Step 1: Form pairs by lining up according to height and forming pairs starting at one end of the line. Ask pairs to take turns interviewing each other, asking:
- What do you do to make sure you are productive while you're studying?
- What can you do to make homework time more fun?

Pull the group together and compare notes. Discuss:

- Why do teachers assign homework?
- What do students learn by doing homework?
- "Search Institute research has found that youth who do at least one hour of homework experience positive outcomes (better grades, etc.). This, however, doesn't address different ages of youth. What do you think is a reasonable amount of time to spend on homework each day for grade school, middle school, and high school?"

Step 2: Comment that the group knows a lot about homework, and has good advice to share with younger students. Have pairs join to form teams of four. Challenge each team to write a "top ten" list of advice and ideas about doing homework that can be shared with these younger students.

Beyond the activity: Recruit volunteers to deliver the lists to teachers or leaders of younger age groups. Also consider submitting this list to your school's newsletter for families or parents.

Why Do Well?

Focus: Youth tell each other why they want to do well in school.

You will need:
- pencils or pens
- self-stick note pads

Set the stage: Give each youth several self-stick notes. Ask them to think of reasons why they want to do well in school and to write each one on a separate note.

Step 1: Invite a volunteer to be the first to read her or his reasons, posting them on a wall or newsprint. This youth chooses the person who will report next. As this youth presents her or his reasons, he or she should post them next to similar reasons from the first person or to start new categories. Continue in this way until all reasons are presented and grouped.

Step 2: Review the main reasons by looking at the groupings on the wall. Ask, "If I asked your parents or other adults at home why they want you to do well in school, which of their reasons would be the same?" Have youth move the notes that have the reasons they think would be the same to a form a new grouping. Then look at the notes that were not moved and ask, "Who or what influenced you to mention these other reasons for doing well?"

Step 3: Ask, "If I asked your teachers and leaders of youth organizations why they want you to do well in school, which of their reasons would be the same?" Again, have youth move the notes that have the reasons they think they would be the same to form a new grouping.

Step 4: Discuss:
- How do families encourage and support your desire to do well in school?
- What do other adult leaders and teachers do to encourage and support your desire to do well in school?
- What is the role of friends and other peers in inspiring you to do well in school?
- Which of these groups is most important to you as you strive in school?

Thumbs Up/Thumbs Down

Focus: Youth reflect on things they care about in their school.

Points to remember: After youth complete the worksheet, ask them to compare their responses in teams of three. Lead a discussion, asking:
- Did any of your "thumbs up" items appear on someone else's "thumbs down" list? Which ones? Why do you think this is so?
- How does your school acknowledge things that are going well or good work that someone does?
- What advice would you give a student who is trying to cope with something on the "thumbs down" list that is really bugging her or him?

How Do You Learn?

Focus: Youth describe ways that they like to learn.

Points to remember: As youth finish, remind the group that this worksheet isn't a scientific instrument; it is meant to give them insights into how they approach a learning task. Ask for volunteers to share how he or she scored, and to say whether it seems to be an accurate description or not. Then ask the group:
- Are most school assignments primarily visual, auditory, or kinesthetic?
- How can you approach an assignment in a way that is good for you to learn, even if the final work will be in one of the forms that isn't your favored one? (For example, can students talk through math problems before writing them down, write an outline to help them organize a project, or try to duplicate experiments described in the book?)
- When a group of students is working on a cooperative project, how can you be sensitive to how other people learn?

Keep Me Motivated

Focus: Youth compile lists of what others say that motivate them to do well in school.

Points to remember: When youth are finished, encourage them to mingle and compare notes. You might ask:
- Who does the best job of motivating you to do well in school? What do they say and how?
- If you were asked to write a list for the parent newsletter of the best things to say to motivate a student, which words and phrases would you include?
- When would be a good time to try some of these comments with a friend or a younger child?

The Ultimate Homework Hangout

Focus: Youth imagine what the perfect home study space would be like.

Points to remember: Allow time for each youth to show her or his idea of Homework Heaven. As a group, note which items seem to be most popular. Ask each youth to tell which three items would be the most helpful to her or him.

If you have completed the How Do You Learn? Worksheet and have time, it may be interesting to see if youth with a certain learning style preference tend to choose similar types of items for their Homework Hangout. Discuss:
- Would your parents or other adults at home agree with the items that you think are most important? Why or why not?
- How might an item that is a distraction for one person be a valuable tool for another?
- How is your current homework space different from your idea of a Homework Hangout?

Wheel of Learning

Focus: Youth recall what they have learned in many settings.

Points to remember: Ask youth to share with the group the items they starred as the most valuable things they learned:

- Where were you when you learned the most valuable things? What criteria did you use in determining what was valuable for you to have learned? If you completed this activity based on the past month instead of the past week, what would change?
- If you asked your parents or other adults at home to complete this wheel, what do you think it would look like? Do you know what they learn from day to day? How could you find out?

You spend a lot of hours in school. What is going great there? Note those things as "Thumbs Up!" What drives you crazy? List them as "Thumbs Down!" Think about the things you write in each list. When things are going great, how do you let others know? When things drive you crazy, what strategies do you have for coping with them or changing them?

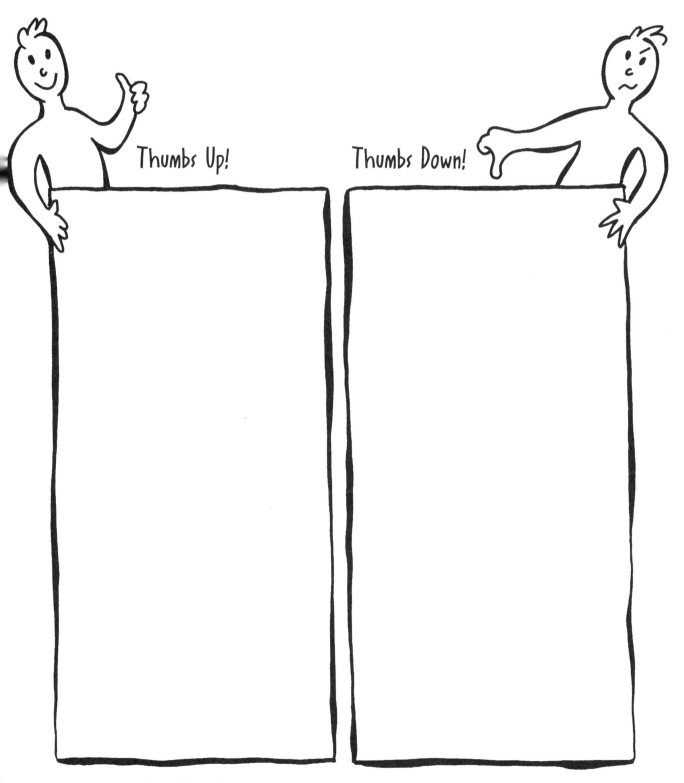

Thumbs Up!

Thumbs Down!

Great news! For your birthday you got a gift card to Everything Electronics, and it's enough to buy that new DVD player you've been wanting. The way you approach this happy task can tell you a lot about how you learn. Choose just one answer for each of the questions below and see what you discover!

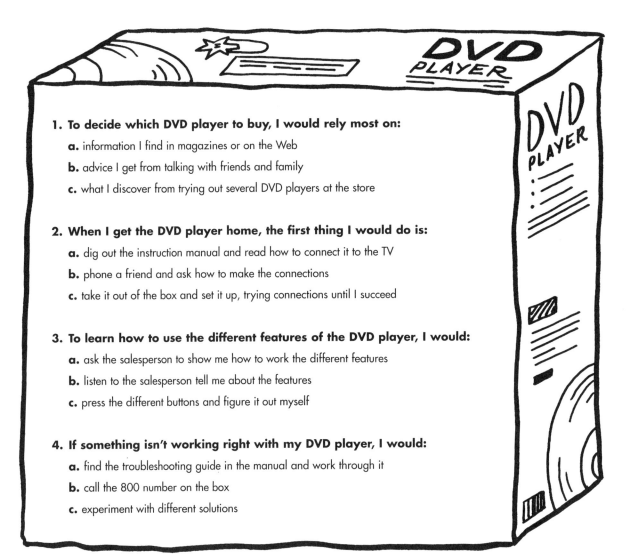

1. **To decide which DVD player to buy, I would rely most on:**

   a. information I find in magazines or on the Web

   b. advice I get from talking with friends and family

   c. what I discover from trying out several DVD players at the store

2. **When I get the DVD player home, the first thing I would do is:**

   a. dig out the instruction manual and read how to connect it to the TV

   b. phone a friend and ask how to make the connections

   c. take it out of the box and set it up, trying connections until I succeed

3. **To learn how to use the different features of the DVD player, I would:**

   a. ask the salesperson to show me how to work the different features

   b. listen to the salesperson tell me about the features

   c. press the different buttons and figure it out myself

4. **If something isn't working right with my DVD player, I would:**

   a. find the troubleshooting guide in the manual and work through it

   b. call the 800 number on the box

   c. experiment with different solutions

If most of your answers are "a," you probably tend to be a **visual learner.** You enjoy reading and it's easy for you to learn from written descriptions, instructions, and charts or graphs. You may like to color-code things as you organize them. When someone demonstrates how to do something, you can then do it yourself.

If most of your answers are "b," you probably tend to be an **auditory learner.** You enjoy discussing information and it's easy for you to learn from conversations with others. You may like to "talk things out" to find the solution to a problem. When someone tells you how to do something, you can then do it yourself.

If most of your answers are "c," you probably tend to be a **kinesthetic learner.** You enjoy being active and moving, and it's easy for you to learn new things by doing hands-on experiments and projects. You may like to draw diagrams or pictures as notes to help you remember information. When you figure out how to do something by trial and error, you can remember how to do it again.

Did you discover that you have some characteristics of each learning style? This is normal, because you have been exposed to many ways of learning in school. Most people, however, have one style that is dominant. How could you use this information about your learning style to help with your schoolwork?

You've probably heard many people talk to you about doing well in school. Which comments are inspiring and really make you want to try? Which words just make you mad or feel like giving up? Take a minute to remember what you've heard and note them in the spaces below. Underline the ones that you've heard yourself say to someone else.

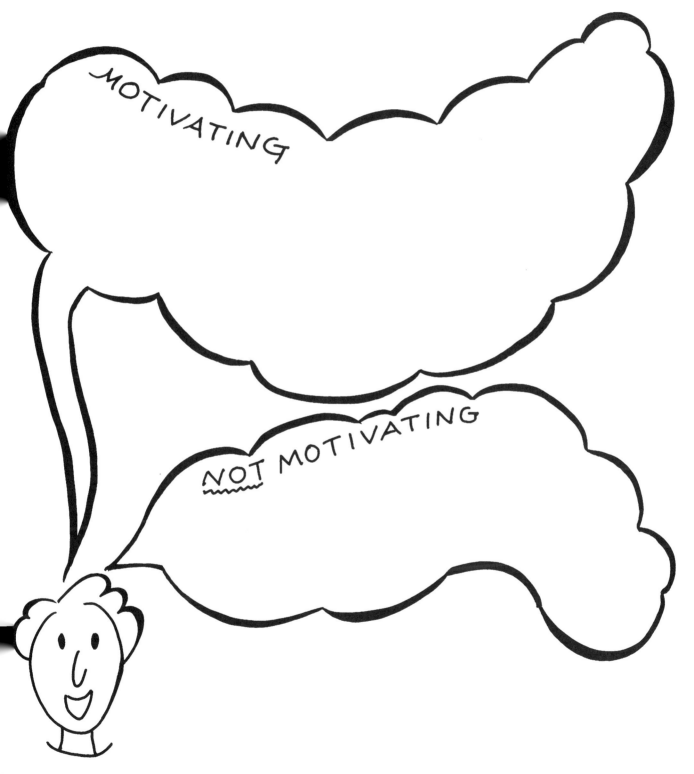

MOTIVATING

NOT MOTIVATING

Imagine the perfect place to do your homework. (You can have all the space you want and spend all the money you want to furnish and decorate it.) Where would you sit? What gadgets would you have? What would make it easier for you to complete your assignments? Sketch your idea of a great place to do homework on the floor plan below, labeling each of the items you would include.

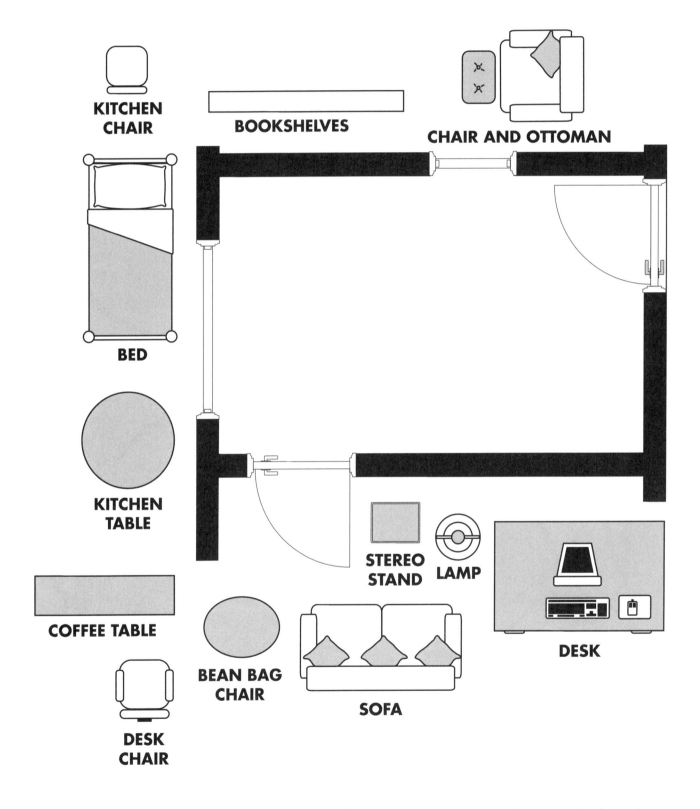

Learning is a lifelong process. Wherever you spend your time, you're always learning something. Of course, some of that learning is more valuable to you than others! Think back to last week. Where did you spend your time? Write each place in a section of the wheel. Next, think about what you did in these places. What did you learn while you were there? Put a star by the three things you learned that are the most valuable to you.

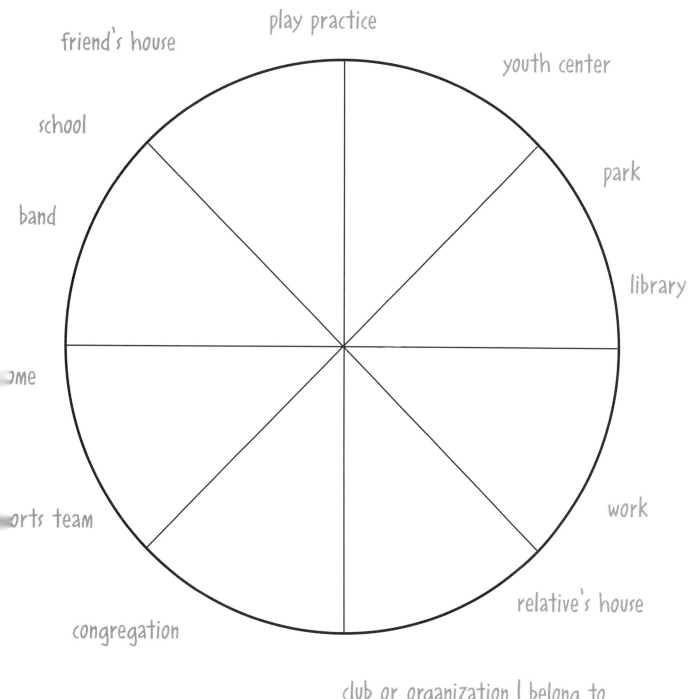

Chapter 7

The Positive-Values Assets

Young people are more likely to thrive when they develop strong guiding values or principles, including caring about others, having high standards for personal character, and believing in protecting their own well-being. These values become an "inner compass" to guide the many decisions and plans that youth make. The activities in this chapter are designed to encourage youth in their commitment to strengthening these assets in themselves and others.

78

Meet a Local Need

You will need:
- Materials to be determined by project that youth choose

Focus: Youth plan and carry out an activity to collect donations for a local agency that serves children.

Note: This activity will take more than one session.

Before the group arrives: Identify a local agency or organization that serves children in your community and inquire about donations it is requesting currently. Ask for information to share about the group, perhaps from a brochure, newsletter, or Web site.

Set the stage: As you introduce the activity, ask youth if any of them have had any experiences with the agency or organization you have selected. Determine what youth know about this agency, and then distribute the information you have gathered. Report what you have learned about the needs of this group. Add that many people who receive various services become adults who give back to that organization and the community.

Step 1: Challenge youth to brainstorm all the possible ways they could work together to supply what this group needs. Come to a consensus on one idea and coach youth in preparing an action plan: who, what, where, when, how.

Step 2: After youth have gathered the needed funds and/or items, arrange a time to visit the agency and deliver the donations as a group. Allow time for youth to visit with the children, if possible, and to ask agency leaders any questions they have.

Step 3: Complete this activity by discussing:
- Were there any surprises in this project? If so, what were they?
- How did this activity help you live out some of the Positive-Values assets?
- What new experiences did you have as you completed this project?
- What new insights did you gain about children in our community?

What's the Message?

Focus: Youth respond to the values presented in media messages.

You will need:

- advertisements cut from magazines popular with youth (include product ads as well as "public service announcements")—five per pair of youth
- markers

Set the stage: Form pairs for this activity by asking youth to find someone else wearing the same color. Give each pair five magazine ads.

Step 1: Challenge participants to think carefully and critically about the words and the graphic images in each ad in order to describe the message they are receiving from it. Pairs should then write on the ad with marker the message that they are receiving. If youth struggle with this assignment, coach them with questions such as:

- What action does the advertiser want you to take?
- What does the advertiser want you to feel about yourself?
- What does the advertiser want you to feel about others?
- What expectation or promise is the advertiser holding in front of you?

Step 2: Ask each pair to present their ads to the group, explaining their reasons for the message they wrote on each one.

Step 3: Spread all the ads on the floor or table in the center of your group. Discuss them, asking:

- Which of these ads are promoting values that are important to you or your family?
- Which of these ads promise to improve something about you? Which are promoting ways to spend your time or money in ways that you think could help you build your self-esteem?
- Which of these ads are promoting something that will help you reach goals that you have set for yourself? Which are promoting something that could hinder your chances of reaching your goal?

80

Best and Worst

Focus: Youth evaluate media messages for their values content.

You will need:

- glue sticks
- magazines popular with youth that can be cut apart
- markers
- newsprint
- red construction paper (or a red marker)
- scissors
- tape

Before the group arrives: Write each of the Positive-Values assets and its description near the top of a sheet of newsprint (leave plenty of open space on the paper). Post these six charts around your meeting space.

Set the stage: As you begin this activity, review the six Positive-Values assets with the group. you have information about your community from Search Institute's *Profiles of Student Life: Attitudes and Behaviors* survey, share the results for these six assets.

Step 1: Form six teams by counting off by six. Instruct all the 1's, 2's, 3's, etc., to form a team. Assign each team to one of the assets. Direct teams to look through the ads in the magazine you have, looking for at least one ad that reinforces, illustrates, or promotes their assigned positive-values asset. Have them cut out this ad and glue it to the asset chart.

Step 2: Ask teams to look for at least one ad that is a negative example—its key message is direct opposition to what is described in the Positive-Values asset they have been assigned. When negative examples are found, teams should make a small "not" sign (a circle with a diagonal line) from red construction paper and glue it to the ad as they put it on the asset chart.

Step 3: After teams have finished, take a walking tour of the charts, encouraging teams to explain their choices. Then ask:

- How much influence do ads have on where and how you decide to spend your money and your time?

- Which are more effective in influencing you—positive ads or negative ads? Why? Do you think this is different for younger youth?
- What can you do to encourage yourself and your friends to make decisions about time and money based on positive values?

81 ———— ## Talk to the Leaders

Focus: Youth communicate with leaders about current events that concern them.

You will need:
- local and national news sections from current newspapers (at least one per youth)
- markers
- newsprint
- tape

Before the group arrives: Make a list of the names, addresses, and e-mail addresses of government leaders for your community or township, state or provincial government, and federal government. Make a photocopy for each youth.

Set the stage: As youth arrive, ask each one to begin looking through the papers for stories about justice and equality issues. Ask youth to circle articles they feel report on the most important issues facing your community and nation.

Step 1: Allow time for each youth to report on one article that he or she circled. Make a list on newsprint of the key issues identified.

Step 2: Discuss tips for effective communication by letter or e-mail messages with a government leader in order to express concern or to share recommendations. Note these key parts of an effective message on newsprint as you present them:
- Use correct name and form of address;
- State the specific event or issue that concerns you;
- Tell why this is a concern—use "I" language to express your thoughts and feelings;
- Say what you hope the official will do (vote a certain way? speak out? study the issue?);
- Say what you will do about the issue (talk with others? correct a problem in your school or neighborhood?);
- Thank the official for her or his time and interest; and
- Keep your letters to one page.

   Ask youth to work individually or in pairs to write and send a letter or e-mail a message about their concern to the appropriate official. Encourage youth to bring copies of any responses they receive to a future gathering of your group.

Variation: This activity could stretch over several weeks so that young people can ask their peers to help them revise their letters.

82 ———————————— **Show a Child You Care**

Focus: Youth plan positive ways to interact with a younger child.

Note: This activity will take several sessions to complete.

Before the group arrives: Write each of these labels on its own sheet of newsprint: Preschool Children and Kindergarten, 1st and 2nd Grade students, 3rd and 4th Grade students.

You will need:
- assorted small toys that younger children enjoy (foam balls, board books, small cars, action figures, dolls, etc.)
- markers
- newsprint
- other supplies as identified by youth

Set the stage: As youth arrive, give each one a toy to play with during the discussion. Introduce the activity by inviting youth to remember the kinds of things they liked to do when they were preschoolers and kindergartners, 1st and 2nd graders, and 3rd and 4th graders. If any youth have siblings, cousins, or neighbors who are these ages, ask them to report on what these younger family members like to do. Encourage youth who baby-sit to relate what they have learned about these age groups. Expand the discussion by asking, "When you were a child, what did adults or older youth do to let you know that they cared about you?"

Step 1: Form three teams of youth. Give each team one of the labeled charts. Tell the teams that they are to write down ideas for caring things they could do for or with children who are the age written on their charts. Challenge teams to think of ways to show the children in their own community that youth care about them.

Step 2: After ten minutes, have each team present its ideas. Ask each youth to star her or his two favorite ideas on the charts. Look at the results together, and decide what your group will do "to show kids you care." Coach youth as they put together an action plan: who, what, when, where, and materials they will need.

Step 3: Center your discussion after the action plan is completed on these questions:
- What did you learn about children as you did this activity? What did you learn about yourself?
- How were you able to be a role model of the positive values of caring and responsibility for each other and for the children? Were there any other positive values that you modeled during the time you spent with the children?
- Is there any follow-up action that needs to occur? If so, what steps do you need to take?

83 ———————————— **Random Acts of Kindness**

Focus: Youth explore the practice of caring as its own reward.

Note: This activity will take more than one session.

You will need:
- index cards or shared computer file
- markers
- newsprint

Set the stage: Write the phrase "Random Acts of Kindness" on a chalkboard or newsprint. Gather impressions from the group on the meaning of this phrase. Ask youth to give examples of such acts that they have done (or have observed) and that others have done for them.

Step 1: Imagine how many random acts of kindness your group could do in one week (such as holding doors open for strangers, helping a sibling with homework, leaving money in the phone coin return cup of a public phone). Tell youth that they will work in pairs to perform anonymous acts of caring for one week. Set a goal for the total number of acts that the group wants to accomplish. Decide on how to record what was done. Pairs could write each act on an index card to bring in or record them in a shared computer file or common Web site. Suggest that youth keep a journal to record the reactions to the acts they performed.

Step 2: After the week is up, report the total number of acts and celebrate reaching the goal. Discuss the experience with a few of these questions:

• What kinds of things did you do? Which were the most fun? Which made you feel most satisfied? Were there any that you wish you hadn't done? Why or why not?

• Were you able to observe any people as they discovered your random acts of kindness? If so, how did they react?

• What did you learn about yourselves as you performed your random acts of kindness? What did you learn about others?

84 — It's a Dilemma

Focus: Youth cooperate to find solutions to a dilemma.

You will need:
• copies of skit starter
• pencils or pens

Before the group arrives: Make a copy of this skit starter for each team of three youth:

> Nate has been struggling in English this year. He's barely keeping the average mark he has to have to play baseball. The test on Friday will "make or break" his semester grade and his place on the team. Nate knows he hasn't studied enough for the test. Mitch says, "No problem. Make sure you sit next to me and I'll feed you the answers you need." Nate thinks back to the Student Honesty Pledge that both he and Mitch signed at the beginning of the year. How does this story end?

Step 1: Ask youth to line up in numerical order by the day of their birth and form teams of three beginning at one end of the line. Give each team a copy of the skit starter and tell them they have five minutes to create an ending to the story and to plan how to act it out, showing what the characters would say and do.

Step 2: After each team has presented its ending of the story, discuss the results:

• What did your story endings have in common? Which ones do you think are the most realistic? Why?

• If you took the best from each of your skits, what solution would you create?

• How do a person's values affect what happens when he or she has to make hard choices?

• What other dilemmas would make good skit starters? (As you have time, challenge teams to present an ending to one of the skit starters they suggested.)

85 — Assert Yourself

Focus: Youth practice being assertive in positive ways.

You will need:
index cards
masking tape
old newspapers
one die
pencils or pens
small treats for winning pair

Before the group arrives: Find a large open area. Tape down sheets of newspaper as the "squares" to make a large game board of at least 30 spaces. (Pairs of youth will walk around the board as the "game pieces.") Designate a start and finish. Be prepared to read each of the scenarios described in Step 2 as certain numbers are rolled.

Set the stage: Ask youth to find the person who has the birthday closest to her or his own. These pairs will be partners for the game. Gather the group by the Start square.

Step 1: Explain the game: Each pair will roll the die and move together that many squares (if the die ends up on 2 or 4 the team misses a turn). As certain numbers are rolled, the leader will read a challenge that the pair must work together to complete before moving. If they can't complete the task, they have to stay in place. The pair that reaches the Finish square first gets the treats.

Step 2: Describe the following scenarios:

- *When a 1 is rolled, say:* "Your teacher makes an assignment that you don't understand. Give an example of what you could say to clarify the teacher's expectations."
- *When a 3 is rolled, say:* "You have damaged an item that belongs to your parent/guardian. Give an example of what this could be. Then, make an apology that includes what you want to have happen next."
- *When a 5 is rolled, say:* "A friend has done something that upsets you. Give an example of what that action could be. Then, make a statement that begins with the words 'I feel' that tells your friend how you feel about the situation and what you want to happen next."
- *When a 6 is rolled, say:* "You and your friend are being considered as lunch hour telephone receptionists at school. You have a meeting with the principal to say why you think you should share this responsibility. Make a statement that includes three reasons why you would be a good match for this position."

Step 3: After the game, talk about the experience:

- What kinds of statements were easiest for you to make? Which were most difficult? Why?
- What makes an effective apology?
- Why is it important to express your feelings when you're upset with something that a friend has done?
- How do you express your feelings to people who aren't your friends?
- How can you talk about your strengths without it sounding like you're bragging?

86 — What Do You Think?

Focus: Youth get to know each other better.

You will need:

- candy (individually wrapped)—20 per youth in sandwich bags
- a list of the Positive-Values assets
- pencils or pens
- writing paper

Set the stage: Explain this activity as an opportunity to learn more about what is important t each member of the group. Take a few minutes to review the six Positive-Values assets.

Distribute paper and pencils and ask youth to write the words "I think it's very important to . at the top of their papers and write the numbers 1, 2, and 3 down the left-hand side. Tell ther that they will have a few minutes to think about how they would complete this sentence with statements that relate to (but do not simply repeat) the six Positive-Values assets.

Step 1: Explain that they need to come up with three ways to complete the sentence, and tha one of the responses should not be true. (It should be something that the youth actually think is not important or is wrong. It might help to mention that this game is a version of "Two Truths and One Lie.") Tell youth that they will play a game later in which other group membe will try to guess which statement is not true, so they shouldn't be too obvious. Tell youth to a star by the incorrect statement. Caution them not to show their papers to each other and t fold them when done.

Step 2: Allow about five minutes for youth to spread out to think and write. Then ask youth gather in a circle with their folded papers. Give each one a sandwich bag with 20 pieces of wrapped candy, telling participants not to eat any.

Step 3: Explain the game: One by one, each youth will turn her or his back to the group and read aloud her or his three statements. The group will have a minute to talk about what they think is true and false, and then the leader will ask for a show of hands to determine which item most youth think is untrue. If the group correctly guesses the false statement, the youth has to give each group member a piece of candy. If the group guesses incorrectly, each group member must give the youth a piece of candy.

After all youth have read their statements, discuss these questions while participants eat their candy:

- What new information did you learn today? What was surprising? Why?
- What are the advantages of knowing more about what your friends and other peers think is important? Are there are any disadvantages?
- What can you do if you and a friend do not agree on important values?

87 — Should I Lie?

Focus: Youth debate whether a lie can ever be the best course of action.

You will need:
- crepe paper (3–4 rolls per team, in two colors)
- marker
- newsprint
- one die
- tape

Before the group arrives: Print this statement on a sheet of newsprint in large letters: "Honesty is not always the best policy."

Step 1: Form two teams by asking each youth to roll the die. Those who roll from 1 to 3 are on one team, and those who roll from 4 to 6 are on the other (teams don't have to be equal in size). Give each team crepe paper and instruct them to create some form of "team uniform" with it. Each team member must wear the team color.

Step 2: Post the chart with the statement for debate. Ask one team to defend this statement, thinking of reasons and examples to prove why it is good advice. Assign the other team to argue against this statement, thinking of reasons and examples to prove why it is bad advice.

Step 3: Give teams about 10 minutes to prepare their arguments and decide who will be first speakers and second speakers for their teams.

Step 4: Use a coin toss to determine which first speaker goes first. Listen to both first speakers, then both second speakers. Time carefully so that each speaker gets only two minutes. At the end of the debate, ask:

- Which team won? Why do you think so?
- Is there a difference between "withholding the truth" and "telling a lie"? Why or why not?
- If a 10-year-old child asked you if it were ever okay to tell a lie, what would you say? Are there different degrees of honesty (lying to spare someone's feelings, etc.)?

88 — Custom License Plates

Focus: Youth create values messages.

You will need:
- easel
- list of the six Positive-Values assets
- markers
- newsprint
- tape
- white construction paper cut to the size of car license plates (one per participant)

Before the session: Jot down any examples you see of "vanity" license plates.

Set the stage: Ask youth if any of their family vehicles have customized or "vanity" license plates. Have youth write the plate messages on newsprint, and ask if the group can tell what the combinations of letters and numbers stand for or mean. Share the examples you have noticed.

Step 1: Challenge pairs of youth to create messages that promote the importance of the six values named in the Positive-Values assets. (Review these six assets as necessary.) Tell pairs they can use a total of nine numbers and/or letters for each license plate they create. Encourage each pair to design at least two license plates. Allow about 15 minutes for pairs to work.

Step 2: As each pair shows its license plates, ask the other youth to guess the message and the related asset. Have pairs explain the thinking behind the message they created.

These creations can be shared with others on a "Road to Positive Values" bulletin board or hallway mural.

89 ─────────────── **Why Not?**

Focus: Youth evaluate restraint messages.

You will need:
- construction paper (red, yellow, green)
- index cards
- pencils or pens

Before the group arrives: Cut sheets of red, yellow, and green construction paper into eighth Each youth needs one piece of each color.

Set the stage: To begin the activity, ask youth to recall messages they have heard that encourage them (or order them!) to refrain from sexual activity, drinking alcohol, or using drugs. Challenge them to think of messages from parents, other adults, organizations they belong to, friends, and the media. Tell them to write each one on an index card.

Step 1: Collect all the cards. Pass out the red, green, and yellow pieces and explain that you will read each message and that each youth will then hold up her or his rating of the message The ratings are as follows:

RED: Stop. Don't say this; it is not effective.

YELLOW: This is okay, but not really motivating.

GREEN: Go for this one. It is motivating.

Step 2: Read each message, pausing for youth to give it their ratings. Remind them that they are expressing their opinions and everyone may not agree. Note on the index card how many ratings of each color are given to each message. (If your group is large, appoint youth to help count each of the colors.) After all the messages have been read and rated, look at the five th received the highest number of red ratings and the five that received the highest number of green ratings.

Step 3: Discuss:
- What do the messages with the most red ratings have in common?
- What do the messages with the most green ratings have in common?
- If your parents or other adults at home were rating these messages, would the results have bee the same? Why or why not?
- How can our group share our top five and bottom five messages with parents, teachers, and o adults?

Responsibility Walk

Focus: Youth consider ways to gain more responsibility.

You will need:
- markers
- newsprint
- tape

Before the group arrives: Write these labels at the top of separate sheets of newsprint: home, school, congregation, youth organization, neighborhood, work. Post these around your meeting area, spacing them as far apart as possible.

Set the stage: Ask youth to think about the various responsibilities they have—things other people are counting on them to do.

Step 1: Invite youth to walk around to each chart and write down key responsibilities they have in the areas mentioned. (Youth do not need to put their names by the things that they write.)

Step 2: As a group, review the items listed on each chart. Focus your discussion with questions like:
- Are there any surprises on these charts? If so, what are they?
- What are the advantages and disadvantages of having these various responsibilities?
- What is the relationship between responsibilities and privileges in these various areas? What do you think about the balance of responsibilities and privileges in your own life?
- Are adults more likely to trust youth who handle responsibility well? Why or why not?
- What advice would you give to a friend who wants to have more responsibility?
- Do you have enough responsibilities? Too many?

Values Reminder Cards

Focus: Youth make pocket reminders of decision-making helps.

You will need:
- index cards
- markers
- newsprint
- tape

Set the stage: To introduce the activity, ask youth to describe the process they go through when they need to make an important decision.

Step 1: Form teams of three. Direct each team to think of five questions they could ask themselves to help them think through a problem and make a decision that would reflect values they think are important. Ask each team to write its five questions on newsprint and then post it in your meeting space.

Step 2: As a group, review each team's work. Encourage youth to ask each other about their reasons for the questions they wrote. Discuss with group members:
- Which of these questions have you ever asked yourself? Which have been the most help to you?
- What advantages are there in taking the time to ask yourself questions like these before you make a decision? What are the disadvantages?
- Is it better to think through these questions alone or with another person, like a friend or family member? Why?

Step 3: Distribute index cards and markers. Tell each youth to choose three or four of the questions that he or she really wants to remember and to write them on an index card to keep in a book bag or on a desk or dresser at home.

Injustice and Me

Focus: Youth reflect on their own experiences with injustice.

Points to remember: The items on this worksheet are primarily for personal reflection. If you choose to discuss some of them, remind the group to use good listening skills as people relate what may be very painful experiences. Do not force any young person to share. There is a blank column included on the sheet where youth can note the responses of others in your group, if your group is comfortable sharing this information. You may want to focus your conversation on how we can care for others who are suffering an injustice and how we can care for ourselves when we feel we have been treated unfairly.
Then ask:
- What's the one thing you would like people to know about you who are under the wrong impression due to misinformation?
- What's the one thing you can do to make sure you don't treat others unfairly?
- Why do you think we treat each other unfairly? What can we do to change that as a group?

Values

Focus: Youth consider the values that are most important in different arenas of their lives.

Points to remember: Ask youth if they added any value statements to the ones on the sheet. Ask youth to share what they are comfortable saying to the group; then ask:
- Why might the values in different areas of your life be different?
- What can you do when the values of one area of your life conflict with the values of another area? How can you decide which values are more important and maintain integrity?

Say It on a Screen Saver

Focus: Youth create a screen saver that presents a positive value they want to promote.

Points to remember: Encourage youth to share their designs with the group, comment on the thinking behind their work. Consider inviting youth to install one of their designs a computer monitor at work or home or tea youth participants how to install them on the own computers.

What Does It Look Like?

Focus: Youth recall how others have demonstrated positive values.

Points to remember: After youth share som of the examples they have observed, ask:
- What can you say or do to encourage othe when you see them doing something positiv
- What have others said to you when you ha been observed doing something good (at home, in school, in the community)?
- What encourages you to do good things?

Pressure Points

Focus: Youth examine daily pressures that they experience.

Points to remember: After youth have a chance to mark the pressures they are experiencing currently, take a poll to see w pressures are most common for your group Invite them to share coping strategies. Ask
- What are the healthiest ways you know to avoid getting stressed out?

Positively Valuable

Focus: Youth reflect on their understanding of values and how it affects the people around them.

Points to remember: Share some examples of how you've made a difference in your home, neighborhood, congregation, or community. Encourage youth who want to share their stories to do so, too. You might ask:
- Why are values important?
- Which values do you think will be most important when you are young adults? Are these different from the values that are most important now? Why?

Have you ever been in a situation in which you were treated unfairly? Have you ever been insensitive or unfair to someone else? Answer each of these items by checking the box that shows how often you have been part of these types of situations. What have these experiences taught you?

How often have you...	Never	1–3 times in my life	At least once a month
Been discriminated against because of your race?			
Made an unfair assumption about someone because of her or his race?			
Been mistreated because of your gender?			
Treated someone else unfairly because of her or his gender?			
Been stereotyped because of your age?			
Disrespected someone because of his or her age?			
Been misunderstood because of your religious beliefs?			
Treated someone else unfairly because of her or his religious beliefs?			
Been looked down on because you were poor?			
Looked down on someone because he or she is poor?			
Mistreated someone because of how he or she looks?			
Been mistreated because of the way you look?			

People are always talking about "values." You may hear the word used by family, friends, and the media, but what does it mean? Think of all the places where you spend time. What are the beliefs that guide your actions in these places? What motivates others to act a certain way in these places? Choose three values that are important to you no matter where you are. Circle the ones that are given, or write your own.

When the monitor of the computer you are using goes to screen saver mode, what are you looking at? What screen savers have you noticed on other people's monitors? Think of a screen saver message and graphics that would remind you and others who see it of one of the six Positive-Values assets. Choose one you think is especially important and design your screen saver here. Then, if you can, install it!

If you need a refresher, the six Positive-Values assets are:

- **Caring**—Young person places high value on helping other people.

- **Equality and social justice**—Young person places high value on promoting equality and reducing hunger and poverty.

- **Integrity**—Young person acts on convictions and stands up for her or his beliefs.

- **Honesty**—Young person "tells the truth even when it is not easy."

- **Responsibility**—Young person accepts and takes personal responsibility.

- **Restraint**—Young person believes it is important not to be sexually active or to use alcohol or other drugs.

"Actions speak louder than words." "Walk your talk." Statements like these remind us that it's important to follow through on what we say. Who has done a good job of *showing* you the meaning of the six Positive-Values assets? What have you seen those people do? Use words or drawings to describe your examples below. Do the people who've done these actions know they have been a good example? How do you let them know?

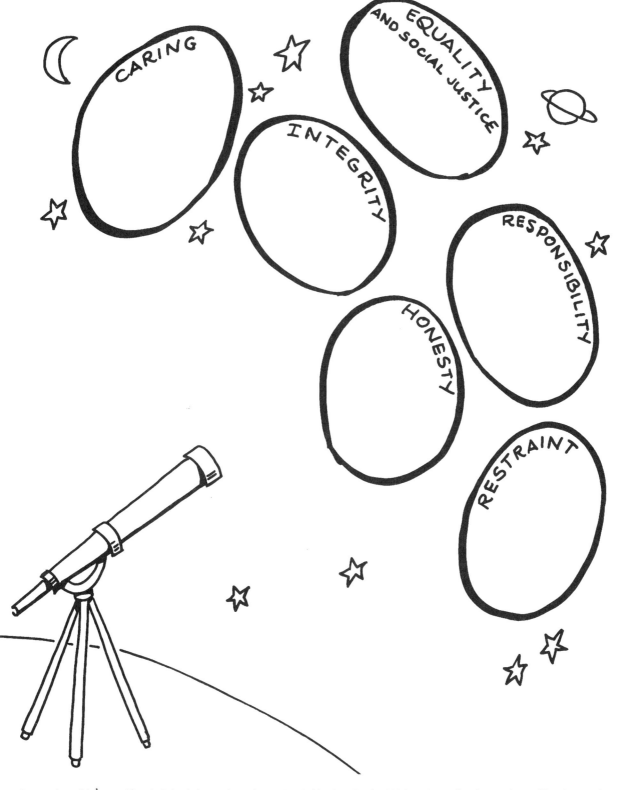

What pressures are you facing? In the American study titled, "The State of Our Nation's Youth 2001–2002," the young people surveyed were asked how much of a problem each of these pressures was for them. How would you respond?

Problem	Major Problem	Minor Problem	Not a Problem	For me, this is . . .
Too much pressure to get good grades	26%	36%	38%	
Too much pressure to look a certain way	16%	30%	53%	
Financial pressure	15%	27%	57%	
Pressure to do drugs or to drink	12%	24%	64%	
Pressure to engage in sexual activity before you are ready	10%	20%	69%	
Loneliness or feeling left out	0%	24%	67%	

Do the results of this survey seem realistic to you? How would your friends have responded?

When you feel the pressure closing in, what are your best strategies for coping?

Which values guide your responses in these situations?

*Source: "The State of Our Nation's Youth 2001–2002," Horatio Alger Association of Distinguished Americans, Inc., 2001.

Do you act on things that are important to you? How? Listed below are the Positive-Values assets. Use the space provided to fill in examples of how you have made or will make an effort to act on each of these six assets.

Caring—Young person places high value on helping other people.

Equality and social justice—Young person places high value on promoting equality and reducing hunger and poverty.

Integrity—Young person acts on convictions and stands up for her or his beliefs.

Honesty—Young person "tells the truth even when it is not easy."

Responsibility—Young person accepts and takes personal responsibility.

Restraint—Young person believes it is important not to be sexually active or to use alcohol or other drugs.

Chapter 8

The Social-Competencies Assets

Young people need to develop the skills to interact effectively with others, to make difficult decisions and choices, and to cope with new situations. Developing these skills will help them live out their values, beliefs, and goals in life. The activities in this chapter encourage youth to consider the importance of these assets.

98

Sweet Idea Exchange

Focus: Youth help each other identify skills for making and keeping friends.

You will need:
• candy (individually wrapped in five colors)—10 pieces per youth
• sandwich bags

Before the group arrives: Put 10 pieces of candy into a sandwich bag (two of each color) for each youth.

Set the stage: As you introduce the activity, comment that the youth in your group have many years of experience in making and keeping friends, and that you'd like them to share their knowledge with each other. Give each youth a sandwich bag of candy. Ask youth not to eat the candy yet.

Step 1: Explain the directions of the game: The goal of the game is to have at least three pieces of candy in each of three different colors. Participants may trade only one piece of candy with a person at a time. Candy cannot be traded until both youth in the trade tell an idea for making and keeping friends.

Step 2: After youth have finished trading, discuss these questions as youth enjoy their candy:
• Where did you learn how to be a friend?
• What does real friendship mean to you?
• What have you learned about how to lose a friend?
• What's the best experience you've had being someone's friend?
• What has been the worst experience you've had being someone's friend?

99

I'm Sorry

Focus: Youth rehearse a method for making apologies.

You will need:
• markers
• newsprint
• tape

Before the group arrives: Write this on newsprint:
  Say what happened and your interpretation of it;
  Add how you feel about the situation;
  Describe what you would like to have happen next.

Set the stage: Ask youth to think back to times when they have had to apologize. Invite volunteers to share their stories, noting what went well with their apologies and what didn't. Call on volunteers to tell of times when others apologized to them, noting how the apology improved or didn't improve their relationship with the person.

Step 1: Show the newsprint, explaining that the letters SAD can be a reminder of how to make effective and caring apologies. Give an example for each letter:

S: I left the burner on and then set a potholder down on it. The fire scorched the finish on the top of the stove.

A: I am so sorry. I should have turned off the burner and I should have been paying attention to where I was putting the potholder.

D: Please forgive me. I'll go to the home store tomorrow and buy a new potholder, as well as something that I can use to clean the stove top.

Step 2: Work through one or two examples as a group (breaking a window with a basketball; saying something mean to a younger sibling).

Step 3: Form pairs. Tell each pair to prepare an apology, using the SAD reminder, for this scenario:

> Friend A promised to go to the movies on Saturday with Friend B, but then forgot all about it and went to play basketball instead. Friend B waited around the theater for an hour on Saturday, then left. When Friend B sees Friend A at school the following Monday, Friend is angry and Friend A suddenly realizes what happened.

After the pairs present their solutions, discuss:

- What steps would you add to or take away from SAD? Why?
- Do you think of being able to make an apology as a skill in building strong relationships? Why why not?
- What can you do if you apologize, but the other person is still angry and won't forgive you?
- What can you do when someone owes you an apology, but does not offer one?

100 ———————— Conversation Circles

Focus: Youth express their opinions on statements about cultural competence.

You will need:

- overhead projector and transparencies if your group is quite large

Step 1: Ask youth to form two circles, one inside the other, with the same number of people (each young person should be facing someone else in the other circle). Spread out to leave plenty of space between people in the circles. Have youth in the inner circle turn and face you in the outer circle, forming conversation pairs. Tell pairs that after you read a statement, they should tell each other whether they agree or disagree with it and why. After the discussion of each statement, youth in the outer circle will move one person clockwise to form new pairs for the next statement.

Step 2: Use these statements, allowing about three minutes for each partner discussion. (If you group is very large and it will be difficult for youth to hear the statements, write them on an overhead transparency and project them onto a screen. Or form two discussion groups.)

- Our cultural heritage is important to my family.
- If people take the time to learn more about different races or cultures, they will be less like to fear them.
- I enjoy learning about my friends' racial or cultural backgrounds that are different from my own.
- My neighborhood does a good job of welcoming people who come from other countries.
- My school doesn't have a lot of tension between racial, ethnic, or cultural groups.
- My teachers have helped me learn about different cultures and traditions.

Step 3: After the discussions, gather as a group and ask:

- What did you hear that was surprising? What did you hear that was reassuring? What did you hear that felt like a personal challenge to you?
- Where there any differences in opinion? How did you handle that?
- Which statements did you agree with most strongly? Which statements did you disagree with m strongly?

• Did your discussions uncover any improvements that you would like to make in your community or your school? If so, what are they? How can our group help to start these improvements?

101 — Violence Is . . . Peace Is . . .

Focus: Youth illustrate definitions of violence and peace.

Note: This activity may take more than one session.

Before the group arrives: Write on newsprint:

Violence: sounds like____;   looks like____;   feels like___.
Peace: sounds like___;   looks like____;   feels like___.

Set the stage: Discuss with the group the images and words they would use to complete the blanks on the newsprint. Brainstorm as many as possible, noting them on the newsprint.

   Ask, "What would you like to teach others about your feelings on violence and peace?" Write these ideas on newsprint as well. Post it where youth can refer to their notes as they work.

Step 1: Decide how to divide the work of creating a bulletin board or hallway mural on this theme with the materials you have brought.

Step 2: After the display is completed, ask: "What questions do you want people or groups to think about or discuss after they see your display?" Write these on newsprint and post them near the display or put them in your organization's newsletter.

You will need:
• bulletin board or mural paper
• construction paper
• glue sticks
• markers
• newsprint
• old magazines and newspapers
• scissors
• tape (or easel)

102 — This Makes Me Angry!

Focus: Youth imagine peaceful solutions to situations that anger them.

Set the stage: Distribute writing paper and pencils. Ask each youth to think about a situation in daily life that makes her or him mad, then to write this situation on the paper (e.g., missing the bus, getting a low score on a test, being teased).

Step 1: When all youth have finished writing, ask them to circulate with their sheets of paper, looking for other youth who wrote down something similar. Youth who wrote something similar on their sheets form a team. (If some youth cannot find anyone with a similar complaint, ask them to form a team of "Assorted Gripes.")

Step 2: Ask each team to write "What has helped" and "What has not helped" on one of their sheets and to take notes while they discuss what they have tried in dealing with their shared gripe. Tell each team to prepare a report to the group that offers advice on what to try and what not to try when others face this type of situation.

Step 3: After the presentations, ask:
• Did these shared gripes have anything in common? If so, what?
• What did the "try this" advice have in common? What did the "don't try this" advice have in common?
• What is one new thing you will try in a situation that makes you angry?

Variation: Refocus this activity and call it "This Makes Me Glad!" Ask youth to think about the things they experience that make them happy or encourage them to keep a positive attitude.

You will need:
• pencils or pens
• writing paper

103 ——————————— Inside Out

Focus: Youth share their own experiences of being included and excluded.

You will need:
• one chair for each youth

Before the group arrives: Place chairs in a circle, with room to walk between each one.

Set the stage: Invite youth to sit in the circle of chairs. Explain that you will read a statement and that their task is to listen, think, and then follow the instructions.

Step 1: Pause for a few moments after each statement for youth to respond and for the group to absorb where various youth are standing. Remind youth to respond quietly, refraining from discussion until the end. Work through all the statements before beginning a group discussion on the activity. Use these statements, adding to them to make the activity meaningful for your community:
• If you ever have felt that you were being treated unfairly because of your gender, stand outside the circle.
• If you ever have felt welcomed by a group of people you didn't know, stand inside the circle.
• If you ever have felt afraid for your safety because of your race, stand outside the circle.
• If you have a friend who has a different cultural, racial, or ethnic background, stand inside the circle.
• If you speak more than one language, stand inside the circle.
• If you ever have felt that you were being treated unfairly because of your accent or language, stand outside the circle.
• If you ever have felt that you were being treated unfairly because of the shape or size of your body or because you have a disability, stand outside the circle.
• If you ever have felt embarrassed by the way your parents/guardians look, speak, or act, stand outside the circle.
• If you ever have felt at home in someone else's congregation, stand inside the circle.
• If you ever have introduced yourself to someone you didn't know, stand inside the circle.

Step 2: After you finish with the statements, stay in the circle and discuss:
• *What surprised you about this activity? Did anything make you feel uncomfortable or sad? If so, what?*
• *What questions would you like to ask each other about your responses? (Allow time for this.)*

104 ——————————— Waiting Game

Focus: Youth share strategies for having patience and making choices that strengthen themselves and their relationships.

You will need:
• construction paper (five sheets)
• marker
• tape

Note: This activity might trigger some unpleasant memories. Be prepared to offer care and support to individual youth.

Before the group arrives: Number the sheets of construction paper 1 through 5. On "1," write "Very Easy." On with "5," write "Very Difficult." Post the five sheets around your meeting space.

Set the stage: As you introduce the activity, ask, "What have you had to wait for today?" After the youth give examples, ask, "In which of these situations was it easiest to be patient? Why?"

Step 1: Explain that you will read several examples of situations that require waiting for something or someone. After each one, youth should decide how difficult it would be for them to be patient in that situation, and stand by the sign that indicates their rating on a scale of 1 to 5—"1" is very easy to be patient and "5" is very difficult. Pause after each one and invite youth to tell what they have tried to make it easier to wait or to be patient in that situation. Use these statements, changing them as necessary to better fit your setting:

- Sitting in the waiting room at the dentist's office.
- Waiting for your score on a test.
- Sitting in a traffic jam on the freeway.
- Waiting for a family member to get ready to leave the house.
- Waiting for a summer vacation trip.
- Waiting to hear if you "got the job."
- Waiting to find out if you made the team.
- Standing in the lunchroom line at school.
- Standing in line to buy concert tickets.
- Waiting for a friend to phone you.
- Waiting for an answer or decision from a parent/guardian.
- Standing in a checkout line at the store.
- Trying to find something in a really messy locker or closet.

Step 2: After responding to all the statements, discuss:

- Which situations seemed to be easiest for our group? Which seemed to be more difficult?
- What tips can you share for making it easier to wait?
- What are the advantages of being known as a "patient person" by your family and friends? What are the disadvantages?

105 —————————————— **Bouncing Back**

Focus: Youth strengthen their ability to recover from poor choices.

You will need:
- balloons in other colors to fill in so that there is one balloon per youth
- five balloons in one color
- small slips of paper

Before the group arrives: Write each of these statements on a separate slip of paper, roll it up tightly, and insert it into one of the five balloons that are the same color:

- You are the *youth with a problem.* Begin the role-play by saying, "I can't believe that Mom found the cigarettes I had in my jacket pocket. What was she doing going through my pockets anyway? Don't I have the right to any privacy at all?" (If you prefer to play the youth with the problem, keep this slip for yourself.)
- Speaker 1: How could you have been so dumb? What were you thinking—leaving them in your jacket? *(Continue with other comments that are accusing and blaming.)*
- Speaker 2: What do you think you need to do? What do you want to happen next? *(Continue with other comments that help the person with a problem think through the situation.)*
- Speaker 3: I'll tell you what you'd better do. You should tell her you were carrying them for a friend and that you won't do it again. *(Continue with other comments that suggest not facing up to the truth.)*
- Speaker 4: Is there any other possibility here? Is there anyone else who could help? *(Continue with other comments that help the person with a problem think about who else might help.)*
    Inflate and tie off all the balloons.

Set the stage: Gather in a circle in an open space. Toss in the balloons. Tell youth to bat them around and see how long they can keep them all in the air. After a few minutes, have each youth hold one balloon. Ask the five youth who have the same color balloons to come to the center of the group.

Step 1: Explain the activity: Inside the five balloons are descriptions of the part each youth will have in a role-play. The role-play takes place at a table in the school lunchroom. The *youth with a problem* will speak first. Then the four speakers will take turns saying their lines (one at a time) and creating a short conversation with the youth. Each of the four conversations will be stopped after one minute. The youth in the audience should evaluate how helpful each of the conversations seems to be for the *youth with a problem.*

Step 2: Tell the five youth to pop their balloons and read their slips. Instruct the *youth with a problem* to begin immediately.

Step 3: After the role-play, ask:

- Ask the *youth with a problem,* "Which of the four speakers seemed to be most helpful to you in thinking about how to bounce back from this situation? Why? Which seemed least helpful? Why? Then ask other youth to share their perceptions.

- Which of these comments have you ever said to yourself in a problem situation? How can talking to yourself help you decide what to do?

- What are the most helpful things you can do to support a friend who is facing the consequences of her or his own poor choice?

106 ——————————— Who's Here?

Focus: Youth investigage demographics in their community.

Note: This activity may take more than one session.

Before the group arrives: Make copies of current, local census data for youth to review. Make sure to include information about population growth (or loss) and the ethnic makeup of your community or neighborhood. Bring this key data for 30 years ago and 50 years ago as well. If you would like to expand this activity, invite a person who works with immigrants in your community to join you for this session to talk about services your community provides to newcomers from other countries and to answer questions.

You will need:

- demographic data for your community (census data should be available from your city, county, or township office or the reference desk at the library. United States census information is available at www.census.gov; the link to "State and County Quick Facts" is especially helpful. Canadian census information is available at www.statscan.ca)
- markers
- newsprint
- reference materials

Step 1: Allow time for youth to look individually through the census data you have provided. a group, discuss interesting or surprising information that they discovered. List where the newcomers in your community have come from and locate these places on a map or globe (if there are any young people in the group who have recently immigrated, invite them to share their experiences). Ask when each youth's ancestors first came to this country.

Step 2: Compare the current information about population changes with the data from 30 and 50 years ago. Ask youth to offer their theories about why these changes have taken place.

Step 3: Form teams of three and ask each one to research one of the places that recent immigrants in your community have come from and to record five key pieces of information about that place on newsprint to share with the group. Provide reference books or access to the Internet.

Step 4: Allow 15 minutes for teams to work. Ask each team to present its five key pieces of information. Then discuss:

- What would be better ways to learn more about different races and ethnicities in our community

- Do you know any recent immigrants? If so, how did you meet each other? What do you have in common? What has been challenging about getting to know each other? (If your group includes recent immigrants, ask them to talk about their experiences of moving into your community and getting to know people.)

- What different reactions to newcomers in your community have you observed in other adults and youth? Which seem helpful? Which seem to cause problems? Why do you suppose people respond to newcomers in the ways that they do?

Faces

Focus: Youth construct a puzzle to encourage cultural sensitivity in younger children.

Note: This activity may take more than one session.

Before the group arrives: Locate a group or class of kindergarten or 1st-grade children who can meet with your youth for about 15 minutes during this activity.

You will need:

- children's magazines
- family-oriented magazines
- large zipper-closure food storage bags
- markers
- permanent markers
- poster board
- small paint brushes or foam brushes
- very sharp scissors (one per team)
- white glue (diluted)

Step 1: Form teams of three. Give these instructions: Find and cut out pictures that show the faces of children and families from many different backgrounds. Plan how you will arrange these on the poster board; then brush glue on the backs of the pictures and place them. Use the markers to add words that will help children learn about getting along with people from different backgrounds such as: be a good listener, share, invite. After the glue is dry, use a pencil to lightly draw the puzzle pieces and cut the poster board into 20-25 pieces and put the pieces in a bag. Brainstorm ideas for how the group might explain these ideas to a younger child. Note that youth might hear things that cause concern. Talk about ways to handle these situations.

Step 2: Meet with a class or group of younger children, having each team of three work with a small group of children to assemble the puzzle on the floor.

Step 3: Encourage older youth to ask children questions about the pictures in the puzzle, and to talk with them about the value of similarities and differences among people.

Step 4: Let the class or group of younger children keep the puzzle for future play. Ask your group:

- What did you learn from the younger children as you put the puzzle together?
- Did you hear anything from a child that concerned you? If so, how did you respond to the child who made the comment?
- What do you think families can do to help their children learn to accept people who are from a different background? What can schools or congregations do?

Find the Word Game

Focus: Youth explore the dynamics of planning and teamwork.

You will need:
- seven index cards

Before the group arrives: Print each of these words in capital letters on an index card: plan, your, work, then, work, your, plan.

Step 1: Form two teams by having youth count off by twos. Explain how this game is played: Team 1 will leave the room while Team 2 hides seven index cards. Team 2 can hide the cards anywhere within the meeting space. When Team 1 returns to the room, they must find all seven cards. If they feel it's necessary, Team 1 is allowed to ask questions that can be answered by a yes or no. Team 2 must take turns answering any questions—a person can only answer one question and cannot be asked a second question until all other members of Team 2 have answered a question. Also, members of Team 2 must tell the truth. Members of Team 1 may speak to each other during the search. Members of Team 2 may not speak to each other.

Step 2: Ask Team 1 to leave the room. Tell Team 2 to hide the cards and to make sure that each team member knows the location of every card. After hiding the cards, ask members of Team 2 to sit in a line so that it will be easier for Team 1 members to remember who gets the next question.

Step 3: Tell Team 1 to return and begin searching. As leader, do not say or do anything. Resist the temptation to end Team 1's search too soon. If you are running out of time, conclude the search 10 minutes before the end of your group time so that you have time for discussion.

- Team 2: What did you learn about teamwork from observing Team 1 trying to find the cards? What did you observe about their planning and decision making? What would have made it easier for Team 1 to accomplish the task?
- Team 1: What did you learn about teamwork during this game? What did you learn about planning and decision making? Looking back, what do you wish you had done before you started?
- Show the words on the cards and ask the group to figure out the phrase you have in mind ("Plan your work, then work your plan"). Ask if any youth have heard this phrase before and where. Ask, "How would it have helped to be given this phrase before you started the game?"

109 ——————————— Hot and Cold

Focus: Youth discuss strategies for sorting through mixed messages.

You will need:

- current magazines and newspapers
- one self-stick note pad

Set the stage: Ask for two volunteers to leave the room. Tell the youth remaining in the room that they are going to play a game like the children's game "Hot and Cold." Assign every other person to help the volunteers, saying "warm, hot, hotter," and so forth as they get closer to the object and "cold, colder, freezing," as they get farther away from the object. Tell the other youth that they are to use the same words, but that their goal is to convince the volunteers to go in the opposite direction from the object. Tell youth that they will be calling out their clues at the same time. Hide the pad of sticky notes, making sure all youth in the room know where it is.

Step 1: Call the volunteers back into the room. Tell them you have hidden a pad of self-stick notes and that their goal is to find it. Say that the other youth will help them find it by saying "hot" if they are close to the sticky notes and "cold" if they are not. Do not say anything else about the instructions you gave to the youth in the room.

Step 2: Give a "go" signal. Resist the temptation to help, clarify, or end the activity too soon.

Step 3: After the sticky notes have been found, ask for two other youth to volunteer to leave the room. Hide the sticky notes in a different location, assign which youth will help and which will mislead, call the volunteers back into the room, and repeat the activity. After the sticky notes have been found, gather the group for discussion:

- Ask the first pair of volunteers: "How did you decide which voices to follow to reach your goal? Did it help that there were two of you? Why or why not?"
- Ask the second pair of volunteers: "What were the advantages of being the second ones to do this? What were the disadvantages?"
- Ask youth who were trying to help: "What made your job easier? What made it more difficult?"
- Ask youth who were trying to mislead: "What made your job easier? What made it more difficult?"

Comment that another name for this game is "Mixed Messages," and that mixed messages are a challenge we all face as we work toward our goals. There are always things that people do or tell us to do that move us in a direction away from what we are expected to do or what we expect ourselves to do. Ask pairs of youth to look through the newspapers and magazine for articles or advertisements that are examples of messages that work against something th families or school expect them to do or that they expect themselves to do. Share these with t group. Ask:

- How can you tell if a story or ad is sending you a mixed message? How can you tell when pec are sending you mixed messages?

- How can the developmental assets help sort out the messages you receive each day?
- What is your best strategy for "testing" the messages you receive from the people you meet and the media?

Friendship Bookmarks

Focus: Youth make bookmarks with friendship messages for younger children.

You will need:
- fine-tipped markers
- 4-by-6-inch *unlined* index cards
- markers
- newsprint
- paper punch
- self-adhesive clear plastic
- yarn scraps

Before the group arrives: Cut index cards into 2-by-6-inch strips, four per youth. Cut self-adhesive clear plastic into 4½-by-6½-inch pieces, four per youth. Cut yarn into 6-inch pieces, four per youth. Locate a children's library, club, or class that would like to receive the bookmarks.

Set the stage: Introduce this activity to youth as an opportunity to share with younger children their wisdom about getting along with others. To prime their thinking, ask:
- In grade school, what did you learn about getting along with others who were different from you? What did you learn about being sensitive to the feelings and beliefs of others?
- How did you learn to make and keep friends? What did you learn about solving arguments in peaceful ways?

Step 1: Form pairs of youth. Ask each pair to think about what is important to teach younger children about making and keeping friends and getting along with others. Challenge them to find a way to say each of these things in eight words or less. Have pairs write their short teachings on newsprint and review the work of the pairs as a group. Add others that group members create during the discussion.

Step 2: Tell youth about the children's group that will receive their advice on getting along with others. Each pair should choose their eight favorite teachings and write them on bookmarks. Remind youth to print messages so that young children will be able to read them, and to add borders or other decorative touches to make them appealing.

Step 3: Demonstrate how to finish the designed bookmarks: Peel protective paper back on the clear plastic to expose one half of the adhesive. Center bookmark on the adhesive. Then, peel off the remaining protective paper and fold it over so that the edges of the adhesive match. Punch a hole in the top and add a yarn tassel.

Ask for volunteers to help deliver the bookmarks. Or, you might arrange for your group to visit the location to distribute bookmarks and read stories to the children.

Asset Builder Check-Up

Focus: Youth rate themselves on their effectiveness as asset builders for younger youth and children.

Points to remember: Before youth do this worksheet, prime their thinking by discussing caring things that older youth did for them when they were children and ways that older youth made them feel important. After they complete the self-inventory, ask which items some youth have never done, and invite other youth who have done these things to give examples of what they have done.

Path to the Future

Focus: Youth generate ideas about what they will need as they work toward a personal goal.

Points to remember: Encourage youth to share the goals that they have. Have youth share the responses they have written in pairs. Afterward, discuss:
• What ways have you found for dividing big projects into smaller steps? What advice can you give each other about setting a timetable to accomplish the steps?
• What are your favorite ways to celebrate when you complete a big project or reach an important goal?

Stressed Out!

Focus: Youth investigate key physical responses to stress.

Points to remember: Form teams of three fo youth to share the kinds of bodily responses they have experienced to the various stresses named on the sheet. Then discuss as a group
• What are the advantages of recognizing the various responses that your body has to stresses? Are there any disadvantages?
• What is your most effective way of coping w stress signals from your body?

What's Good about Saying No?

Focus: Youth consider the positive outcomes of resisting negative influences.

Points to remember: Go around the circle and ask youth to share their favorite and mo effective ways of saying no. Keep going arou until there are no new ways to add. Form pa and ask each pair to create a miniskit to demonstrate one of the situations they nam on the worksheet and one of their ways to s no. After the skits ask, "What would you tel young child about the importance of being a to say no and to stick by what you say?"

Fair or Unfair?

Focus: Youth learn principles for communicating during a disagreement ("fair arguments").

Points to remember: Items 1, 3, 4, and 5 are the "unfair" statements. Challenge pairs to rewrite them using the guidelines on the worksheet. After pairs have shared their rewrites, continue the exercise by reading the following statements and having youth decide how to restate them so that they are "fair arguments":

- You're never going to convince me of that, so just shut up!
- Nobody likes me! Not even you! (said while crying)
- Why do you always make such a mess in the kitchen?
- Stop what you're saying right now and listen to me!

If you have time, ask youth to share things that they have said or heard during an argument and let the group practice restating them into "fair arguments."

Listen to Me!

Focus: Youth explore ways to improve their skills as caring and effective listeners.

Points to remember: Form teams of three for youth to share what they have written on their worksheets. Ask each team to plan a way to demonstrate one of the careful listening skills. After each team presents, ask:

- What are the advantages of having good listening skills? Are there any disadvantages to being a good listener? If so, what are they?
- Have you ever heard the saying, "A person has two ears and one mouth for a reason"? What does that mean to you?

A Good Citizen

Focus: Youth realize the qualities of citizenship that they possess.

Points to remember: Before youth do the worksheet, review the Social-Competencies assets as needed. Also, ask the group to define the word *citizen* and to describe what they think are important qualities of citizenship. Be sensitive to the variety of comments and emotions that this discussion may elicit (e.g., not feeling connected to the community, not trusting community leaders). Remind youth to practice their listening skills as they learn from each other. After the worksheet is complete, invite youth to tell about the people they listed as role models of good citizenship.

My Friendship Circles

Focus: Youth identify benefits of various kinds of friendship.

Points to remember: After youth complete the worksheet, have them share their responses with the group. See if your group can make any generalizations about the different kinds of friends that we have in our lives. Ask: "If a young person feels that he or she does not have enough close friends, what advice would you give? How would your advice be different for finding more social friends or more acquaintances?"

111 — **Asset Builder Check-Up**

It's exciting to dream about the future and make plans for the great things you will do. As you consider your future, think about the other people who will be there—as neighbors, coworkers, friends, and residents in the same community. Your skill as an asset builder with children and younger youth today will affect the quality of your community today and tomorrow! Evaluate yourself on these asset-building actions. Consider how to incorporate more asset building for children and younger youth into your plans for each day.

Name_____

Asset building action	I do this every day	I do this at least once a week	I do this at least once a month	I have never done this
I smile and say hi to children and younger youth when I see them.				
I am a role model of caring language and positive actions for children and younger youth.				
I attend games or concerts of young people I know and cheer for them.				
I keep my eyes open for children while driving or riding my bike.				
I encourage younger people to join in when I'm helping others.				
I help children and younger youth learn or practice new skills.				
I sing or read to young children.				
I ask younger people to be caring and responsible.				
I appreciate the talents and abilities that children and younger youth have— and tell them so!				

Where are you headed? Describe one of your personal goals in the signpost below, then answer the questions in the footprints as you consider the journey you will take to get there.

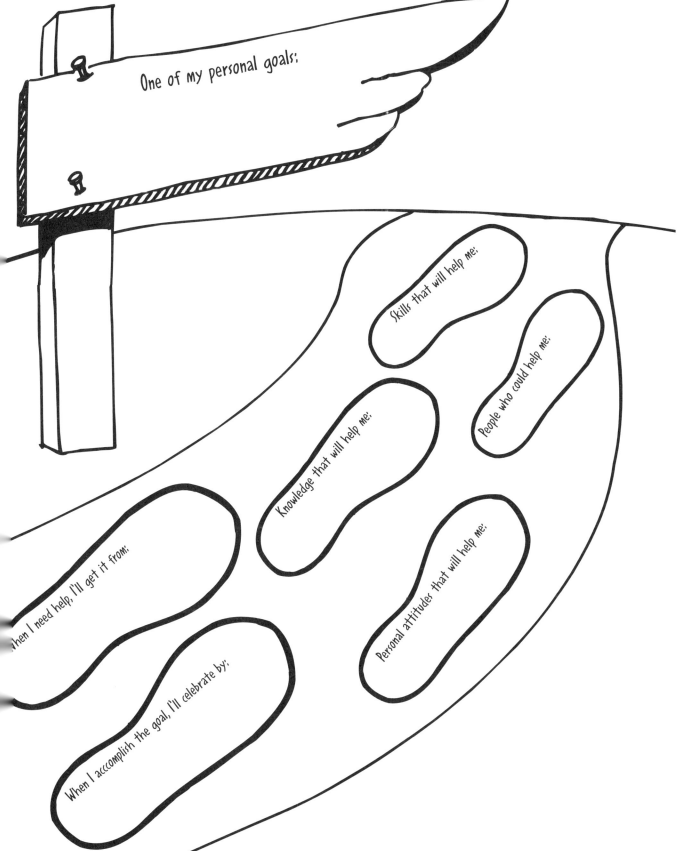

One of my personal goals:

Skills that will help me:

People who could help me:

Knowledge that will help me:

Personal attitudes that will help me:

When I need help, I'll get it from:

When I accomplish the goal, I'll celebrate by:

As a baby, you probably cried when you felt scared, crabby, or anxious. Now that you're older, there are other ways for you to express feelings such as fear, anxiety, embarrassment, anger, or stress. Your palms might sweat, your heart might race, your face might get red, or you might feel sick to your stomach—these are all signals or inner cues that are triggered when you feel a certain emotion. Child psychiatrist Dr. Bruce Perry has studied how we respond to these brain messages and body signals. He explains that as a person matures, her or his ability to stop and think before acting on raw emotion is a lot easier. The bottom line? It's really up to you to decide how you choose to react in certain situations.

Think about the things that stress you out (some examples are listed below). What are some positive ways to handle stress? Describe them below.

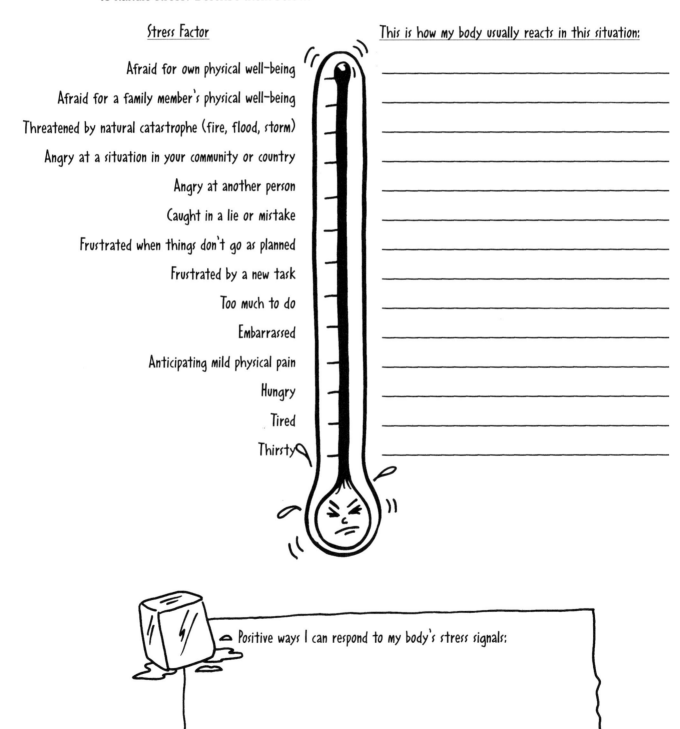

Stress Factor

Afraid for own physical well-being

Afraid for a family member's physical well-being

Threatened by natural catastrophe (fire, flood, storm)

Angry at a situation in your community or country

Angry at another person

Caught in a lie or mistake

Frustrated when things don't go as planned

Frustrated by a new task

Too much to do

Embarrassed

Anticipating mild physical pain

Hungry

Tired

Thirsty

This is how my body usually reacts in this situation:

Positive ways I can respond to my body's stress signals:

"No!" Sometimes it's just what you want to hear. (Has the trip been canceled? Does Grandma have cancer?) Sometimes it's a dreaded response. (Did I make the team? Did I pass the quiz?)

Sometimes no is the most important thing you can say. So it pays to be prepared for when it might be your best response to someone's request and to be creative in thinking of how you can say it. Of all the different things people will ask you and pressure you to do, which ones are sure to get your no? Describe the five situations when you think it is most important to say no in the NO below. In the exclamation point, write your best five ways of saying no.

There are positive and helpful ways to disagree with a friend or family member. Think of these as "fair arguments." There are also times when you can say the wrong thing to someone you disagree with and make the situation worse. Think of these as "unfair arguments."

Decide whether the statements the birds are making below are fair or unfair and circle your choice. Some of the guidelines for being fair as you work through a conflict are also listed below. Try your hand at rewriting the unfair statements to show a better way. Use the back of this page if you need more room.

Everyone appreciates a person who will listen in caring ways. You can learn to be a great listener. Consider your current use of the listening skills listed below. Write down an example of what you would say to a friend using these skills.

Keep good eye contact with the other person, if it is respectful in your culture to do so.

I need to do this more often | I usually do this

When I'm doing this, I might say:

Pay attention to what is being said without words: how a person is sitting, what a person is doing with her or his hands and feet, tone of voice, eye contact. Observe the feelings behind the words.

I need to do this more often | I usually do this

When I'm doing this, I might say:

Restate what the person has said to check your understanding—"It sounds to me like . . . Am I correct in hearing you say . . ."

I need to do this more often | I usually do this

When I'm doing this, I might say:

t's not convenient to listen when a person wants to talk, ure out a time and place to have the conversation.

to do this more often | I usually do this

en I'm doing this, I might say:

en carefully to the words the other person is saying. Avoid temptation to think ahead to what you want to say next.

to do this more often | I usually do this

en I'm doing this, I might say:

Don't offer advice unless the other person asks for it. Sometimes people just want to express their feelings to another person; they aren't looking for a problem solver.

I need to do this more often | I usually do this

When I'm doing this, I might say:

The Social-Competencies assets are attitudes and behaviors that help you get along with the people you encounter each day. Many of these same attitudes and behaviors help you and others in your community and nation be good citizens. If you need a refresher, these assets are:

- **Planning and decision making**—Young person knows how to plan ahead and make choices.
- **Interpersonal competence**—Young person has empathy, sensitivity, and friendship skills.
- **Cultural competence**—Young person has knowledge of and comfort with people of different cultural/racial/ethnic backgrounds.
- **Resistance skills**—Young person can resist negative peer pressure and dangerous situations.
- **Peaceful conflict resolution**—Young person seeks to resolve conflict nonviolently.

Who has done the best job of showing you what a responsible member of the community does? Write their names in the first list. Think about the people you respect at home, at school, and in your neighborhood. What types of things have you learned from them? What qualities do you share? Write these in the second list.

People who are responsible members of the community:

Qualities I share with them:

(border text: VOTES · OBEYS TRAFFIC LAWS · DOESN'T LITTER · COMMUNICATES WITH LEADERS · PROMOTES EQUALITY · CARES ABOUT NEIGHBORS · VOLUNTEERS · RESPECTS OTHERS)

My Friendship Circles

All friends are not the same. You may have some very close friends. You probably have some social friends—other youth you do things with once in a while. As you think about classmates or other youth in your community, some of them are probably just acquaintances—other youth you know, but who aren't part of your social life. Answer the questions below to consider how each of these groups is an important part of your life.

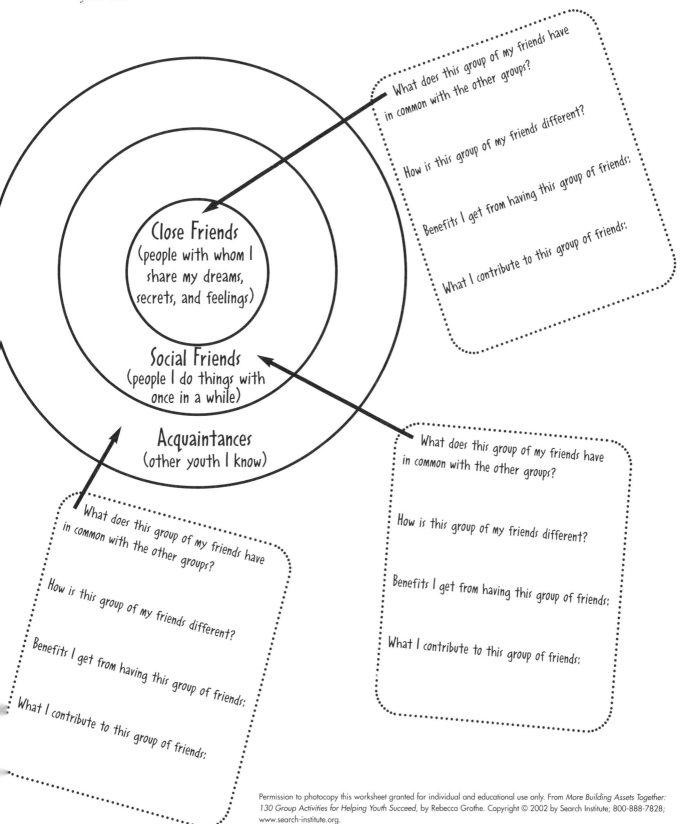

Close Friends
(people with whom I share my dreams, secrets, and feelings)

Social Friends
(people I do things with once in a while)

Acquaintances
(other youth I know)

What does this group of my friends have in common with the other groups?

How is this group of my friends different?

Benefits I get from having this group of friends:

What I contribute to this group of friends:

What does this group of my friends have in common with the other groups?

How is this group of my friends different?

Benefits I get from having this group of friends:

What I contribute to this group of friends:

What does this group of my friends have in common with the other groups?

How is this group of my friends different?

Benefits I get from having this group of friends:

What I contribute to this group of friends:

Chapter 9

The Positive-Identity Assets

Young people need to believe in their own self-worth, to feel that they have control over the things that happen to them, and to have a sense of purpose in life. These assets work together to help youth hold a positive view of their future. The activities in this chapter will help youth consider their own sense of power, purpose, worth, and promise.

119 — Is . . . Isn't

Focus: Youth discern elements of a healthy self-esteem.

You will need:
• index cards

Before the group arrives: Write each of these phrases on a separate index card, changing them as necessary to fit your setting:
• Help others
• Take pride in appearance
• Wear fashionable clothes
• Big allowance
• Have goals for my future
• Talk to myself in negative ways
• Talk to myself to encourage and plan
• Stand up for what I believe
• Let others know my feelings
• Live within my budget
• Feel good about completing a tough assignment
• Take risks
• Allow myself to make mistakes
• Show care and affection for others
• Follow my conscience
• Accept responsibility
• Accept my strengths and weaknesses
• Belong to the "in" group
• Listen to others
• Never apologize
• Insist on having my own way,
• Own state-of-the-art electronics

Set the stage: As you begin the activity, ask youth to define "self-esteem" and to tell about where they have heard and discussed this term. Explain that in this activity, they will consider which life experiences contribute to a healthy self-esteem. Sit in a circle if possible. Youth will take turns drawing a card, reading it to the group, and deciding if what is named on the card is or isn't contributing to a healthy self-esteem.

Step 1: Designate two piles in the center of your circle, one for "is contributing" and one for "isn't contributing." If a youth in the group does not agree with the choice, he or she can call out "debate!" At that point, pause for youth to express their opinions on both sides of the issue.

Step 2: After youth have responded to all the cards, ask:
• Of all the items on the cards, which do you think are the most important? How do the media promote these ideas? How do the media discredit them?
• What can youth do to encourage their friends and younger children to have a positive self-image?

Focus: Youth wrestle with the dynamics of change.

You will need:

- construction paper (red, green, blue, and yellow— several sheets per person)
- marker
- newsprint
- scissors
- tape

Before the group arrives: Write and post this list on a sheet of newsprint:

> Red = Alone
> Green = With one other person
> Blue = With family
> Yellow = As a community

Cut the construction paper into fourths. Each youth needs one piece of each color.

Set the stage: Sit in a circle of chairs or a circle on the floor. Introduce this activity by soliciting comments from youth: "What are some of the areas in which you would like to see change for the better? How does change happen—in your own life, in your family, and in our community?"

Step 1: Point out the color code chart and distribute the construction paper pieces. Explain that you will read several situations in which change is desired. After each situation is read, youth should choose which of the four people or groups named on the chart has the most realistic chance to make the change take place—who has the "power" to make this change happen? Youth then place their piece of the corresponding color on the floor in front of them (if youth are seated in chairs, they can hold up their color of choice and keep the other pieces of construction paper on their laps).

Step 2: Use the following situations, changing them as needed to better fit your setting. Pause after each situation to ask volunteers to give their reasons for their color choice:

- You want to lose weight and get in shape.
- You want to stay out late.
- You want a safer place to skateboard.
- You want to change the curfew law.
- You want a better place to do your homework.
- You want homeless children to attend school.
- You want more things to do on Friday night.
- You want more customers for baby-sitting.
- You want drivers to obey the speed limit in your neighborhood.
- You want media to consider youth opinions in their coverage of local events.

Step 3: After completing the response activity, discuss the dynamics of change by asking:

- What factors do you consider when you're deciding if a certain change is within your power or not?
- What are the advantages of asking others to help make a change? What are the disadvantages?

21 ———————————— **Dearly Departed**

Focus: Youth imagine what might be said of their lives at age 100.

You will need:
• highlighters
• obituaries from newspapers
• pencils or pens
• writing paper

Before the group arrives: Cut out newspaper obituaries of people who died at an old age. Try to find ones that tell about things those people contributed to the community during their lifetimes.

Step 1: Form pairs and ask them to read through several obituaries, using a highlighter to mark important things the person did during her or his life. As a group, report on the contributions these individuals made to the community.

Step 2: Ask youth to imagine what their obituary might say if they were to die at age 100. Allow time for youth to think about this individually, then to outline the key points that might be in their obituary.

Step 3: Invite volunteers to tell the group about their obituaries, but do not force anyone to share. Discuss:
• Why do newspapers print obituaries?
• Was this activity comfortable or uncomfortable for you? Why?
• Of the accomplishments and contributions you named in your obituary, which ones are you working toward already? Which ones are goals that you have yet to start working toward?

Variation: Instead of using obituaries, use a collection of articles (or a video presentation) that recognize people in the community for their achievements. Or ask youth to write down five things they would like fellow members of their community to say about them when they are 100 years old.

22 ———————————— **Morale Boosters**

Focus: Youth plan to encourage and thank others.

You will need:
chart markers
fine-tipped markers
newsprint
tape
3-by-4-inch self-adhesive notes

Before the group arrives: Post several pieces of newsprint around your meeting space. Divide tablets of notes into minitablets of about 10 sheets each. Each youth needs one minitablet.

Set the stage: As youth arrive, invite them to take a chart marker and list phrases or words they use when they want to encourage someone on newsprint posted around the room. Allow time for them to mingle and discuss this with each other, adding to the charts as new ideas emerge.

Step 1: Distribute the minitablets and fine-tipped markers. Have youth decorate each of the sticky notes with a favorite "word of encouragement" from the charts. When they finish, take time to review their work.

Step 2: Challenge youth to use all of their notes during the next week, leaving them for friends, family members, teachers, employers, coaches, and others to find.

   When your group meets again, ask for reports of how it felt to leave the notes and any reactions they observed.

123 ———————— **Gift Chain**

Focus: Youth display the strengths and resources they offer.

You will need:
- construction paper in a variety of colors
- gel pencils or pens in a variety of colors
- scissors
- tape
- thin cardboard or poster board

Before the group arrives: Make several cardboard patterns of an outline of a person with outstretched arms. Make the figure at least 8 inches tall. You may be able to use a gingerbread cookie cutter as a guide for the pattern.

Set the stage: As you begin, ask, "Is it easier to tell other people about your strengths or your weaknesses? Why is that?"

Step 1: Explain that this activity is an opportunity for youth to take pride in their own strengths and to learn more about the strengths of others in the group. Ask each youth to choose a color of construction paper and cut out an outline, using the patterns you've provided. Instruct them to use gel pencils or pens to write this phrase on one side of the figure: "My strengths are . . ." and then to list three answers. On the back of the figure, they can write their names and add any artistic touches that they desire.

Step 2: Gather in a circle and ask volunteers to share what he or she listed as personal strengths. Affirm each person. Pass tape around the circle, having youth tape their figures together at the hands. Hang this chain of "strong people" in your meeting space. Discuss:
- Why is it important to be aware of your own strengths?
- How can youth encourage each other to use their strengths and gifts?
- What is an effective way to respond to a friend who is putting herself or himself down?
- How about a friend who is always boasting or bragging?

124 ———————— **Bragging Rights**

Focus: Youth act out ways to celebrate personal victories.

You will need:
- index cards

Before the group arrives: Write each of these scenarios on a separate index card. You need one scenario for each pair, so duplicate some if necessary.
- You have been chosen for a part in the spring play.
- You score 26 points in the last basketball game, your personal best.
- You finish your term paper a week early.
- You get accepted to the college you want.
- You make the honor roll spring semester.
- You are named employee of the month at work.
- You pass your driver's license exam on the first try.
- You succeed in getting a fire going during a rainy camping trip.

Set the stage: To begin the activity, comment that part of the joy of life is celebrating personal victories as they come along. Ask:
- When you are very happy about something you have accomplished, what do you do or say? What have you seen others do?
- How do you decide if it's a good idea to celebrate a personal victory with others?

Step 1: Form pairs of youth. Have each pair draw an index card, telling them that it describes personal victory. Explain that each pair will prepare a short skit that presents a "Do this" and

"Don't do this" example for how a person could celebrate the moment. Encourage them to be creative and to enjoy imagining all the ways a person could celebrate the event on their card.

Step 2: After each pair presents their dos-and-don'ts skit, begin a discussion by asking:

- Have you ever felt awkward celebrating something good that has happened to you? If so, what happened?
- How can you celebrate with a friend when the very thing that is a joy for her or him is a disappointment for you (such as he or she passed the driver's exam and you didn't, or he or she got the lead in the play and you didn't)?

25 — A Better Place

Focus: Youth create a mural or bulletin board to illustrate their vision for the future.

You will need:
- brushes
- list of the developmental assets
- markers
- mural paper
- newsprint
- tape
- tempera paints

Set the stage: Review with youth the 40 developmental assets. If you have community data from Search Institute's *Profiles of Student Life: Attitudes and Behaviors* survey, take a look at how many youth report experiencing each of the assets. Ask: "What would it look like if our community (or school or organization) took asset building seriously? What would we see happening three years from now?"

Step 1: As youth respond, note their ideas on newsprint for reference while they are working on the mural.

Step 2: Form pairs and assign each pair one section of the mural or bulletin board. Direct them to choose one of the "visions" named during the discussion and paint or draw how they imagine that scene. Suggest they use drawings of people, symbols, words, or a combination of these to express the vision. After pairs are finished, ask for volunteers to paint or draw transitions/borders to complete the space in a visually interesting manner.

Beyond the activity: After admiring the finished work, discuss how this vision can be shared with community and organization leaders. Recruit volunteers to carry out this communication.

Variation: Try this activity outside. Give youth sidewalk chalk to create their mural.

26 — Time Capsule

Focus: Youth put together a "time capsule" to capture their hopes and dreams.

You will need:
- computer with word processing software and printer
- envelopes

Before the group arrives: Check the index of your local paper or search the Internet for examples of groups who have buried or opened time capsules in that past year or so. Bring this information for the group.

Step 1: Begin by briefly summarizing the articles you located about time capsules as you circulate them for youth to see. Ask:

- Have you ever helped create or open a time capsule? Tell us about your experience.
- If we prepared a time capsule for our group, what would you want people to know about each person? What would you want them to know about our group? What would you want them to know about your dreams for the future?

Step 2: Explain that your group is going to create a computer time capsule—with words only. Start a word processing file, and ask for volunteers to summarize information about the group to start the document. Then list the names of the group members and ask each youth to write two or three sentences about her or his hopes and dreams for the future.

Step 3: Print a copy of the file for each youth. Tell youth to put the document in an envelope and label it with their name and the date of their 21st birthday. Encourage them to save the envelope in a place where it will be safe until their 21st birthday. Suggest that they may want tell a parent/guardian about the document to help them remember that they have it.

You're a Card!

Focus: Youth present positive information about themselves.

Points to remember: Take time to admire the completed cards as a group. Challenge youth to discover one new thing about each group member. You may want to make a bulletin board display of these worksheets.

A Thousand Points for Life

Focus: Youth prioritize aspects of their future.

Points to remember: After youth have time to think about what they would like to have in their lives, ask teams of three to compare sheets with each other. Discuss:
• Was this activity easy or difficult? Why?
• How did you decide what to choose?
• How can friends support each other in working toward important goals, even if they are different from each other?

Taming the Critic Inside

Focus: Youth transform negative self-talk (or inner-voice messages) into positive alternatives.

Points to remember: After youth finish editing the statements on the worksheet, poll the group to see how many different ways each statement was changed. Discuss:
• What phrase of healthy self-talk do you say to yourself most often? What is the least healthy?
• How have the things you say to yourself helped or hindered you in the past?
• What is one new phrase of healthy self-talk that you want to start using?

My Life This Month

Focus: Youth choose a positive focus for the upcoming month.

Points to remember: After youth make their choices of short-term goals, invite volunteers to tell the group what they circled and why. Challenge each youth to think of a concrete step to take to begin working toward each goal that he or she circled. If you want to expand this activity, have youth write down the steps they will take and then have pairs check in with each other once a week to share progress reports.

Think back to all the collector cards you have seen. What interesting pieces of information did you learn from them? If you were on a collector card, what would other people learn about you? Fill in the card below and add a photo or drawing of your smiling face.

Name:
Date and place of birth:
Positions held in life:

HIGHLIGHTS

Life highlights:_____

Likes to learn about:_____
Favorite music: _____
Favorite food: _____
Favorite color: _____
Words to live by: _____

A Thousand Points for Life

Imagine what it would be like if you could order the life you want on an Internet shopping site! You have a gift card worth 1,000 points. You have to spend it all to choose the things you want in life, but you can't overspend. Mark which things you would click into your "life cart."

1,000 POINTS FOR LIFE

	Your Cost	Add to Cart	Total
Ten really good friends	100 points	☐	_____
A big house with all the latest electronics	100 points	☐	_____
A loving spouse	100 points	☐	_____
A healthy son or daughter	100 points	☐	_____
Belonging to a meaningful faith community	100 points	☐	_____
A college degree	100 points	☐	_____
An exciting career	100 points	☐	_____
A job with good pay and benefits	100 points	☐	_____
A jet ski or snowmobile	100 points	☐	_____
A new car of my choice	100 points	☐	_____
Good personal health	100 points	☐	_____
A vacation each year to the place of my choice	100 points	☐	_____
A good relationship with my parents	100 points	☐	_____
A chance to make a difference in the life of another person	100 points	☐	_____
A great wardrobe	100 points	☐	_____
Money to give to my favorite charities and causes	100 points	☐	_____
An item of my choice:_____	100 points	☐	_____

TOTAL: 1,000 POINTS

Have you talked to yourself lately? Most people do, you know, though most try not to talk to themselves out loud in public! Healthy self-talk can help you craft the solution to a problem, motivate yourself to keep trying, or help you practice something important that you want to say to another person. Unhealthy self-talk is like a critic in your head. These messages can tear down your self-esteem and even prevent you from trying new things.

This personal player needs a new CD! Edit these negative self-talk messages into healthier ones—more like the ones you would want to tell yourself. There are some tips for changing negative self-talk coming out of the earphones.

My Life This Month

Personal goals can be short term or long range. Sometimes it's tempting to think only about the big goals, but what you will try to do this week or this month are also important goals. Consider your life in the next four weeks. Circle three of the goals listed below that you would like to work toward in the upcoming month. What steps can you take to make sure you accomplish them?

About the Author

Rebecca Grothe has developed resources and training for children, youth, and their leaders for more than twenty years, with an emphasis on resources for volunteers who lead groups of children and youth. While much of her professional experience has been in the congregation sector, she also has worked with youth in her community as an HC • HY Officer for Lutheran Brotherhood and a volunteer in local schools. She is an experienced workshop leader.